GET TΩ THE END

A Catholic's View of the End Times

Michael Hickey

University Press of America,® Inc.

Lanham • Boulder • New York • Toronto • Plymouth, UK

Copyright © 2016 by University Press of America,® Inc.
4501 Forbes Boulevard, Suite 200, Lanham, Maryland 20706
UPA Acquisitions Department (301) 459-3366

Unit A, Whitacre Mews, 26-34 Stannary Street,
London SE11 4AB, United Kingdom

Library of Congress Control Number: 2015960658
ISBN: 978-0-7618-6733-3 (pbk : alk. paper)—ISBN: 978-0-7618-6734-0 (electronic)

♾™ The paper used in this publication meets the minimum requirements of American
National Standard for Information Sciences Permanence of Paper for Printed Library
Materials, ANSI/NISO Z39.48-1992.

I would like to thank my family for encouraging me to write this book and I hope in some small way this will be a legacy of my Christian faith which I will leave with them after I come to my own earthly end.
I would also like to thank my theology faculty advisor and "spiritual father," the late Reverend Daniel Harrington S.J., for sharing his spirituality, intelligence, and biblical knowledge with me as a Master of Divinity student at Weston/The Boston College School of Theology and Ministry. This book is dedicated to the memory of Fr. Dan, who was one of the most humble, wisest, and kindest priests I had ever known.
He had a great sense of humor and a brilliant mind.
I was blessed to be no more than a thirsty sponge in his presence.
He truly was an inspiration to me as he gradually revealed himself to be a vibrant temple of the Holy Spirit.

"All the World's a Stage

And All the Men and Women

Merely Players . . ."

—William Shakespeare, "As You Like It," Act II, Sc. VII

Contents

Chapter One

What Is Omega?

Omega (Ω ω) means literally, "The Great O," and it is the last letter of the Greek alphabet. It signifies finality or the end of something. In Judaism, it was common to use the first and last letters of the Hebrew alphabet to denote the whole of anything from beginning to end. Like "The Great O" any whole forms a complete circle.

Any statement of complete eternality and finality can apply only to God. In the Old Testament Scriptures, through the mouth of the prophet Isaiah, the Lord will tell us early on in Israel's history that it is He who is "the first and the last." For example:

> "I, the Lord, am the first and with the last I also will be" (*New American Bible*, Isa. 41:4).

> "Thus says the Lord, Israel's King and redeemer, the Lord of Hosts; I am the first and I am the last; there is no God but me" (Isa. 44:6).

> "I, it is I who am the first, and also the last am I" (Isa. 48:12).

In our own English language if we wanted to discuss the first and the last, the beginning and the end, we would probably say that it goes from A to Z. On the other hand, the early Christian community lived in a Hellenistic world which understood things in terms of Greek language and Greek culture. In fact the New Testament was written in Greek, thus it used the Greek alphabet from beginning to end.

Alpha and Omega are the first and the last letters, respectively, of the Greek alphabet. The letters Alpha and Omega have been employed from the fourth century on as a symbol expressing the confidence of Christians in the scriptural proofs of Our Lord's divinity and God's eternity. The symbols

1

were also used in early Christianity and appear in the Roman catacombs. Apocalyptic language is often allegorical and employs extensive use of symbols. The particular symbol of the Alpha and Omega was suggested in the Apocalypse/ The Book of Revelation written by the Apostle John, where Christ as well as the Father, is "The Alpha and Omega," "The First and the Last," "The beginning and the end."

The claims to the divinity of Christ as the Son of God, who is the Alpha and Omega are found in the following verses in the Apocalypse/The Book of Revelation:

> "Do not be afraid. I am the first and the last, the one who lives. Once I was dead, but now I am alive forever and ever" (Rev. 1:17).

> "The first and the last, who once died, but came to life, says this . . ." (Rev. 2:8)

> "I am the Alpha and the Omega, the beginning and the end" (Rev. 21:6).

> "I am the Alpha and Omega, the first and the last, the beginning and the end" (Rev. 22:13).

So, only God can be the first of all things and the last of all things. There was no one before Him. So then, Alpha refers to the beginning and Omega refers to the end, but it should be noted that the two are intimately connected and intertwined. There can be no end point without a beginning point, nor can there be a beginning point without an end point. All beginning and end points are determined by the Lord of the beginning who is the same Lord of the end.

GETTING TO THE BEGINNING OF THE END

My wife, Theresa and I, on a visit to the Greek Islands in 2014 had the privilege of visiting the cave on the rocky Greek island of Patmos where the Apostle John, the Evangelist and writer of the 4th Gospel is purported to have written the apocryphal book of Revelation in cooperation with one of his disciples somewhere between A.D. 81–96. Patmos is an island in the Aegean sea and John was exiled to Patmos, as the early church was undergoing a time of persecution under the Roman rule of Domitian. Back then, Patmos was a Roman penal colony. Since John was a contemporary of Jesus, John would have been by that time, well over 90 years old when he wrote the Book of Revelation, making him very likely the only Apostle to survive to such an old age. Amazingly, there is much preserved in that cave just as it was when John prayed, wrote, ate, and slept there in the first century A.D.

The Book of Revelation is one that is pertinent to all times; to the time it was written in the first century of the Christian church as well as to the present and the future end of times. In many ways, it can be seen as an allegory for any and all times for those living in a time of crisis, especially for those on the spiritual path in their ongoing struggle between good and evil.

The cave itself is now incorporated at the bottommost part of a Greek Orthodox Christian church, St John, the Evangelist. It was indeed a moving spiritual experience for both my wife and I to descend the many steps and to be in that sacred, mystical, and holy place where John and one of his disciples wrote the words to Revelation after seeing a vision of Jesus and hearing him say:

> "I am the Alpha and the Omega, the one who is and who was and who is to come, the almighty" (Rev 1:8).

Those words resonated in my heart as we viewed the nearby harbor out of an open stone-encased window just as John viewed it from that very same cave. As we walked in the cave centuries later in his footsteps, we saw the rock hewn altar at which he prayed and viewed the hard rock pillow on which he rested his elderly head to sleep as he waited for the end of his earthly life.

The purpose of this book will be to discuss the Omega point; the end point, which because it is in the unknown future can only be discussed to the extent that the Holy Spirit guides the writer. All of us participate in a collective consciousness and a future memory, whereby we have a partial consciousness concerning the future and the end point of time and history as we know it.

Furthermore, we are told in the Gospels to, "read the signs of the times" (Matt. 16:3). Therefore, this book will try to *GET TΩ THE END*, to the extent my own spirituality, personal knowledge, Catholic/Jesuit formation, and very limited view of the horizon beyond the harbor allows.

Chapter Two

The Eschaton

WHAT IS ESCHATOLOGY?

'Eschata' is also taken from the Greek and means "last things." Therefore, eschatology is that area of theology which is directly concerned with the study of the last things or the end time. If theology, to use St Augustine and St. Anselm's century's old definition, is "faith seeking understanding," then eschatology can be similarly described as "hope seeking understanding."

We work against the virtue of hope by despairing (anticipating failure) or presuming (anticipating success). Eschatology is not merely a hope for the future, because a future that leads to nothingness or sameness is no more than a hope for the present to continue on into time and history. Eschatology, will then involve drastic change and will imply a future which is outside of time and history; it will not be strictly determined by temporal or historical factors. In eschatology (hope seeking understanding), God is not only "above" us, but also "ahead" of us at the end of time and history as we know it. This end point is often referred to as "The Omega Point." God, as the Absolute last thing, will usher in as the fulfillment of a divine plan for the world, the establishment of a new order.

Many books have already been written about the end time. Fewer have viewed the end time from a Catholic perspective. This book will view all of the "last things," strictly from the perspective of a Catholic writer. The last things would include not only death, judgment, heaven and hell, but also a final struggle between God and the powers of evil, salvation, the second coming of Christ, and the resurrection of the body.

So, the Absolute last thing or "Eschaton," is God, both the end and the beginning of all created reality. The Kingdom of God in its final manifestation will ultimately reconcile, renew, and unify all things in the end through the love of God.

The eschaton has essentially begun already with the birth, death, and resurrection of Jesus Christ. So, in many senses, we are in the end time now and our future is wrapped up in the future of the risen Christ who is not only with us now in Spirit, but also ahead of us, awaiting us at the Omega Point.

According to the scriptures, before the end of times, there is foreseen a cosmic upheaval, the collapse of the visible world, and the collapse of human institutions as a prelude to many of the last things. At that time, God will begin a new world and a new age. God will be King and reign supreme.

OLD TESTAMENT ESCHATOLOGY

In the Old Testament, Yahweh (I Am Who Am), as the instrument of judgment, finds its expression in the expectation of 'The Day of Yahweh;' which is the expectation of a cataclysmic encounter between Yahweh and the powers of evil. Eschatological chaos and the upheaval of nature, reminiscent of the days of Noah and the flood, will be the necessary condition for a newly created world. Yahweh will bring this about as the Lord of nature. Yahweh's holiness demands the fullness of a new creation which will be a witness to his righteousness and power and will usher in his universal reign.

Old Testament eschatology seems to have developed first along the lines of a higher and fuller doctrine of immortality and later as apocalyptic imagery, thought, and language and the promise of an afterlife. At first, the recognition of individual responsibility and retribution is confined chiefly to this life. This principle is repeatedly recognized in the earliest books and runs throughout the Prophets and Psalms. For example:

> "Far be it from you (Lord) to do such a thing, to make the innocent die with the guilty, so that the innocent and the guilty would be treated alike! Should not the judge of the world act with justice?" (Gen. 18:25)

> "The Lord answered, 'Him only who has sinned against me will I strike out of my book" (Exod. 32:33).

> "Fathers shall not be put to death for their children, nor children for their fathers; only for his own guilt shall a man be put to death" (Deut. 24:16).

> "He who practices virtue and speaks honestly, who spurns what is gained by oppression, brushing his hands free of contact with a bribe, stopping his ears lest he hear of bloodshed, closing his eyes lest he look on evil, he shall dwell on the heights." (Isa. 33:15–16).

"I, the Lord, alone probe the mind and test the heart, to reward everyone according to his ways, according to the merit of his deeds" (Jer. 17:10).

"For all lives are mine; the life of the father is like the life of the son, both are mine; only the one who sins shall die" (Ezek. 18:4).

But, later on in the Old Testament, we find in the Psalms, Proverbs, and in the book of Job the clear expression of a hope or assurance for the just; of a life of blessedness after death. Here is voiced, the inner craving of the righteous soul for everlasting union with God. The entire problem is dealt with throughout the book of Job and we find it threaded throughout such Psalms as 15, 16, and 17.

"Ill gotten treasures profit nothing, but virtue saves from death" (Prov. 10:2).

"Virtue directs toward life, but he who pursues evil does so to his death" (Prov. 11:19).

"When a man has died, were he to live again, all the days of my drudgery I would wait, until my relief should come" (Job 14:14).

"But as for me, I know that my vindicator lives, and that he will at last stand forth upon the dust; Whom I myself shall see: my own eyes not another's, shall behold him, and from my flesh I shall see God; my inmost being is consumed with longing . . . know that there is a judgment" (Job 19:25–26, 29).

In the Old Testament, the resurrection of the body is implied because of the beliefs held in Pharasaic Judaism. It is also believed that Ancient Israel developed these thoughts from their ties to Canaan. The later Christian doctrine of the resurrection and life after death first finds definite prophetic expression in the Old Testament Books of Isaiah, Daniel and Ezekiel.

"But your dead shall live, their corpses shall rise; Awake and sing, you that lie in the dust, . . ." (Isa. 26:19).

"Many of those who sleep in the dust of the earth shall awake: some shall live forever, and others shall be an everlasting horror and disgrace" (Dan. 12:2).

"Thus says the Lord God: O my people, I will open your graves and have you rise from them, O my people" (Ezek. 37:12).

Finally, as it relates to the Hebrew scriptures, eschatology (last things), can particularly be seen as the expectation of a future eon discontinuous with the present, in which the circumstances of history will be swallowed up and transformed as the present cosmos is redeemed by God. In the closing chapters of Isaiah, believed to have been written much later by disciples of the prophet Isaiah, there also appears to be hints of a developing belief in resurrection and talk of Yahweh creating a "new heaven and earth" as a vista beyond the present veil following all the "last things."

> "Lo, I am about to create new heavens and a new earth; the things of the past shall not be remembered or come to mind" (Isa. 65:17).

> "As the new heavens and the new earth which I will make shall endure before me, says the Lord, so shall your name and your race endure" (Isa. 66:22).

CATHOLIC/CHRISTIAN ESCHATOLOGY

Death

> "The last enemy to be destroyed is death" (1 Cor. 15:26).

Death should certainly be considered as eschatological or among one of the "first things" to be considered when discussing the "last things." Also, if experience is always the best teacher, then certainly writing about death and experiencing our own death must be considered two very different things. It's an old hackneyed saying, but still so true that, "Everyone wants to go to heaven, but nobody wants to die." As is the case with many people, the end of our lives will come unexpectedly and take many of us by surprise. The best thing we can do then is to live every day as if it were our last one because some day it really will be our last day on earth.

Death is a final limiting earthly horizon for all humanity. One way in which it can be understood is as the dictionary describes it as "the termination of all biological functions that sustain a living organism." Because it is a part of life it can be viewed essentially as the termination of one's earthly life. But, because death involves the human person as a whole and is a personal, individual, and spiritual phenomenon, it must be seen as more than the mere cessation of biological processes.

Although we can never know the exact when and where about our own death, the knowledge of our own eventual death and its inevitability determines the whole of our life. Death can be seen as the most tangible expression of our finitude as human beings. However, it is our belief as Christians, that life points us beyond death. The daily scripture guide I read each morning, *the Magnificat*, reassures me often, "We are dust, but we are beloved dust." Through Jesus death, he not only found life, but also opened up a new path to life for the world. At the point of our death, time, space, and history as we know it will end and eternity will begin.

Christian tradition gives a provisional description of death in the phrase "separation of body and soul." This implies that the spiritual principle of life as it exists in a human being, man's "soul," assumes in death a different relationship to what we commonly call the "body." However, this appears to create a duality and it should say much more than this in order to treat a human being as a wholistic spiritual being concerning his or her total "essence." What should simply be said then in terms of Christian belief is that in death there is no cessation of the soul, only a transformative change in its relationship to its previous embodiment and then subsequently a transformative change in the soul's relation to the cosmos and to God.

Although in the face of death, we ourselves are powerless,

> Jesus revolutionized the meaning of death. He did so with his teaching, above all by facing death himself. "Dying he destroyed death," says the liturgy of the Easter season. "With the Spirit that could not die, Christ defeated death that was killing man," wrote a Father of the Church (Melito of Sardis, "On Easter," 66). In this way, the Son of God wished to share our human condition to the end, to open it to hope. Ultimately, he was born to be able to die and in this way to free us from the slavery of death. The Letter to the Hebrews says: "that by the grace of God he might taste death for everyone" (2:9). (Benedict XVI)

Even those who will be found alive at Christ's second coming will experience some form of death in the way of a radical change and transformation in order to inherit eternal life as death's sting is swallowed up in the victory of Jesus Christ.

> "Behold, I tell you a mystery. We shall not all fall asleep, but we will all be changed, in an instant, in the blink of an eye, at the last trumpet. For the trumpet will sound, the dead will be raised incorruptible, and we shall be changed. For that which is corruptible must clothe itself with incorruptibility, and that which is mortal must clothe itself with immortality" (1 Cor. 15:51–53).

The authentic death, which one must fear, is that of the soul, called by the Book of Revelation "second death." In fact, he who dies in prideful rejection of God's love, excludes himself from the Kingdom of life by his own doing. The second death initiates an eternal damnation.

> "Then death and Hades were thrown into the pool of fire (This pool of fire is the second death.) Anyone whose name is not found in the Book of Life was thrown into the pool of fire" (Rev. 20:14–15).

> "But as for cowards, the unfaithful, the depraved, murderers, the unchaste, sorcerers, idol-worshippers, and deceivers of every sort, their lot is in the burning pool of fire and sulfur, which is the second death" (Rev. 21:8).

In Jesus' dying and rising, the entire universe became Christocentric. The world as a whole and as the scene for all the actions of humanity became different from what it would have been if Christ had not died. Christ's death became a determining feature of the entire cosmos; the inmost center of all created reality; it became the heart of the universe which now beats along with our own hearts. For we believe that to die with Christ is to live with him (Rom. 6:8).

Finally, we can be as certain of our own eventual death as we are of Christ's death before us. We should not fear our own death, however, if we have faith in Christ and our intent in this life is to please the Lord. Otherwise, we should not only fear just our own death but fear moreover the judgment seat of Christ. Paul's Letter to the Corinthians tells us:

> "although we know that while we are at home in the body we are away from the Lord, for we walk by faith not by sight. Yet we are courageous, and we would rather leave the body and go home to the Lord. Therefore, we aspire to please him, whether we are at home or away. For we must all appear before the judgment seat of Christ, so that each one may receive recompense, according to what he did in the body, whether good or evil" (2 Cor. 5:6–10).

We can never know with full certainty if at the time of our death our earthly lives will have pleased the Lord or what will ultimately happen to us as we come before the judgment seat of Christ. For now, we can only persevere in faith, while at the same time recognizing that the manner in which we have lived out our earthly journey in this life is what will accompany us into the next:

> "I heard a voice from heaven say, 'Write this: Blessed are the dead who die in the Lord from now on.' "Yes," said the Spirit, "Let them find rest from their labors, for their works accompany them (Rev. 14:13).

Particular Judgment

Most of us want our lives to have counted for something. We want our earthly lives to have had ultimate and final meaning and purpose. Although we certainly have a cosmic and communal destiny in this regard, we also have an individual and personal destiny. At the end of our human life, we will be responsible individually and personally before God for the life we have lived on this earth and the individual person we became at the end of our lives. We have a particular identity and a particular final destiny on this earth. Ultimately, each of us will also have a particular judgment before God.

Death on earth puts an end to our human life and closes the time which was open for accepting or rejecting the opportunity for grace which is manifest in Christ who will be our judge:

"Nor does the Father judge anyone, but he has given all judgment to his Son" (John 5:22).

However, most of the New Testament writings speak of another judgment, the final judgment, which is an encounter with Christ at the Parousia, his Second Coming. Particular judgment, according to Christian eschatology, is the Divine judgment that a person who dies undergoes immediately after death, in contradistinction to the general judgment (or Last Judgment) of all people at the end of the world. This will be discussed under the different heading of "Final Judgment" later on.

Some of the New Testament writings do affirm that there will be, in fact, a particular judgment after death where we will be rewarded according to our works and faith during our earthly sojourn. This will take place before the judgment seat of Christ.

> "Just as it is appointed that human beings die once, and after this the judgment" (Heb. 9:27).

> "What profit would there be for one to gain the whole world and forfeit his life? Or what can one give in exchange for his life? For the son of man will come with his angels in his Father's glory, and then he will repay everyone according to his conduct" (Matt. 16:26–27).

Christ represents Lazarus and Dives as receiving their respective rewards immediately after death. They have always been regarded as typical examples of the just man and the sinner (Luke 16:19–31). Also, to the penitent thief it was promised that his soul instantly on leaving the body would be in the state of the blessed:

> "Amen, I say to you, today you will be with me in Paradise" (Luke 23:43).

Earthly death is an unrepeatable act that ends a person's human life. And just so, Christ's offering of himself and his earthly life is an unrepeatable sacrifice that has once for all achieved redemption for us. Each of us will receive our particular judgment at the moment of our earthly death and at this time, our life will be referred to Christ. We will be judged on our faith and works on earth and as the song goes "They will know we are Christians by our love." So, at that time, as St. John of the Cross and others also have said, "We shall be judged on our love" as well. (St. John of the Cross, Dichos 64, quoted in *Catechism* 1022)

> "So faith, hope, love remain these three; but the greatest of these is love" (1 Cor. 13:13).

Heaven/Eternal Happiness

In most every culture, death is not seen as an extinction. Very often there is some belief in a kind of existence after death both for the righteous and the damned. Only the perfectly pure, righteous, and holy can enter heaven. For those who by the grace of God, find themselves there in God's realm the place may be called heaven, eternal happiness, paradise, beatific vision, or something else, but it is seen as the fulfillment of our deepest longings and a state of supreme happiness or blessedness. The Gospel writer Matthew calls it, the Kingdom of Heaven:

> "At that time, the disciples approached Jesus and said, 'Who is the greatest in the Kingdom of Heaven?' He called a child over, placed it in their midst, and said, "Amen I say to you, unless you turn and become like children, you will not enter the Kingdom of Heaven" (Matt. 18:1–3).

As God's children, heaven is also seen as the place where we can be in communion with God and find joy and happiness in his presence:

> "You will show me the path to life, abounding joy in your presence, the delights at your right hand forever" (Ps. 16:11).

By his life, death, and resurrection, Jesus has opened up the path to heaven for us. It has become a blessed community of saints for all who believe in Christ and who love him and are loved by him. Scripture imagines this as a wedding feast with Jesus as the bridegroom. It is our union with Christ which transfers us to the heavenly realm:

> "I am going to prepare a place for you. And if I go and prepare a place for you, I will come back again and take you to myself, so that where I am you also may be. Where I am going, you know the way" (John 14:2–3).

In heaven, we complete the goal of our human existence as we become fully like God and see him as he is in all his glory; no trace of our human selfishness or egocentric longing can remain. We are no longer as we were on earth, "imperfect saints." Only the perfectly holy, perfectly loving, and perfectly righteous can be in the heavenly realm with the Lord.

Purgation or an Intermediate State

Purgatory or an intermediate state is viewed pretty much as a thoroughly Catholic concept. As a Catholic, I accept the teaching as reasonable, true, and valid. Some of the Christian churches align themselves with this theology and some do not. There are some scriptural references which could be seen as describing it, but they are not fully clear and thus it is more the evolved thinking of Catholic doctrine and Tradition. The main scriptural basis is rooted in the Old Testament book of 2nd Maccabees, Chapter 12, where prayers and sacrifices for the dead are requested for the expiation of sins. The reality is, however, that this scriptural reference shows something similar to the concept of Purgatory, but is not exactly the same.

The Fathers of the early church, Origen in particular, argued for its existence as an intermediate state, but it was not until the 12th century that the doctrine came into prominence. At the time of the Middle Ages, the Western churches saw it as part of God's judgment, while the Eastern churches saw it in a more mystical light. It was seen by the Eastern churches as a process of cleansing, purgation, purification, maturation and spiritual growth to prepare souls for entrance into the purity and holiness of heaven. Several church councils which followed tried to strike a balance between the two perspectives. The Council of Trent in 1565 finalized the theology of purgation as a doctrine of the church.

Purgatory is not an actual place; it is a state of being. The term does not indicate a special location as much as a condition of existence. If Purgatory didn't exist, many of us would have to either go straight to hell, or have become someone other than who we were at the time of our death without any memory of our earthly life.

So, the theological concept of purgatory can certainly get complicated. But, one thing is certain we cannot enter heaven without being cleansed of all impurity, unholiness, or any other form of sinfulness within us. The only thing that is a little uncertain and might be open for debate is how that happens.

Perhaps the best way it should be viewed is first by admitting to ourselves that we are sinners and often selfish. I have a friend that always tells me jokingly: "The only way you can be above sin, is to rent an apartment above a sinner." In addition, we are also, occasionally unloving, unforgiving, and unkind toward others. Isn't there always a certain amount of pain involved in our moving from self-centeredness to Christ-centeredness? With this in mind, we then must also admit that, although we are forgiven, there is no way we can come into the full presence of God after we die and become one with him without being purged and cleansed of this. Only at the point of our death will we know fully how that happens as we face our particular judgment.

On the other hand, if we just automatically assume that we are always pure, loving, righteous, and holy before God all the time, we should get some second opinions right away because chances are we are delusional and in big trouble not only with the Lord, but with our own conscience as well. Unfortunately, in our human condition, even the most prudential and practical judgments as matters of conscience, can be in error. A perfect God insists on our complete perfection and a holy God insists on our complete holiness.

Nothing else will do and no one can come into God's presence and see him face to face otherwise. The Lord told us early on in the scriptures:

"Be holy, for I, the Lord your God am holy" (Lev. 19:2).

Even though God forgives us, we must be in a state of grace to be in communion with God in heaven. That implies that we cannot carry with us any impurities, imperfections, or earthly baggage into heaven from our life in this world. Only God knows our hearts, our inmost being; and the Lord knows us even better that we know ourselves. We cannot always be certain of our motivation or intentions.

There may have been times during our earthly sojourn when we were certain we were doing the right thing, but we may have been doing the right thing for the wrong reasons. For example, we know that it is a good thing to give alms to the poor. If our intention was to give alms to the poor because they need help and to help them we know is a good and Christian thing to do, then our intention is pure and we are in a state of grace. But, if we give alms to the poor because we want to be seen and we want other people to know it and to praise us, then our heart is not in the right place and our actions are not pure. Only God knows this and only God can cleanse us of our sinful nature and make us perfect. God is holy and we must be made holy to be in his presence, in communion with him, and see him face to face. The Gospel confirms for us that we must have the proper motivation in our hearts:

"When you give alms, do not blow a trumpet before you, as the hypocrites do in the synagogues and in the streets to win the praise of others. Amen, I say to you, they have received their reward" (Matt. 6:2).

Just speaking for myself, I know I have a long way to go to become "holy (wholly) perfect" before God. We don't have to be totally and completely wicked to be impure and imperfect. For now, the earthly journey is my focus, not Purgatory, and not the goal of heaven. There are two reasons: First, because by focusing on the journey, I can focus on my changing and not my perfection. Secondly, any perfection or holiness (whole-iness) that I will eventually have will be more attributable to God's holy victory than my own doing. It is best to be present where you are and also to be assured that you are always and at all times somehow mysteriously in the grace of God's presence who loves us as we are.

Hell

In the Old Testament, there is no mention of hell specifically. But, typically the word used to describe anything remotely similar to hell is 'sheol.' In the New Testament, there are three words used, 'gehenna,' 'hades,' and' tartaros,' and even though they can all be translated as 'hell,' they all mean something a little different. What they all have in common is that they all describe a place where none of us would like to end up at the last. Most often they describe a place of eternal punishment or damnation. I get gooseflesh just thinking about it.

By the end of the fifth century of the Christian church, the Athanasian Creed promulgated the existence of hell as a place of eternal punishment for sins and by the twelfth century, a few church councils had taught that those who died in mortal sin went immediately to hell.

The Catholic Catechism, more recently, gives quite a bit of space to the discussion of hell, describing those who either do not love God, those who sin gravely against God, or those who fail to meet the needs of the poor, as those who go there. Hell is seen as a free choice and a place of self-exclusion by those who are unrepentant and remain separated from communion with God eternally. Separation from God is seen as the chief punishment. God, however, predestines no one to go to hell. It is seen strictly in terms of a free choice made through turning away from God in a willful and unrepentant manner. Therefore, the Catechism of the Catholic Church defines hell not as punishment imposed on the sinner, but rather as the sinner's self-exclusion from God (*Catechism,* 1033–37, 269–270).

The scriptures reassure us:

> "The Lord is patient with you, not wishing that any should perish but that all should come to repentance" (2 Pet. 3:9).

Neither Jesus in the gospels, nor the early Christian church of the New Testament, ever states that people actually go to hell or if anyone is actually there in hell. It is only mentioned that the possibility of this exists if someone rejects God fully and completely and makes the choice for a separated and isolated existence apart from God. Neither the New Testament nor the tradition of the Christian church tells us in so many words that any particular person is in hell and Jesus' words regarding hell may be seen as more of an admonition rather than a prediction. Hell is absolute isolation and a rejection of being through the freedom to choose non-being. Therefore, hell is not as much a place we go to and certainly not a place we are sent to by God as much as it is a state of being/non-being we have chosen. God only yields to our free will. God tells us from the outset in the book of Genesis that it is not his desire for us to be alone and isolated:

> "The Lord God said, 'It is not good for the man to be alone" (Gen. 2:18).

In closing, on the subject of hell, I would like to say that it lies beyond the scope of our most vivid imagination as human beings. We can only create

metaphors and other imagery to describe its potential horror as a final existence and ultimate reality. Thinking about hell should make us tremble and
any continuous dwelling on it should make us very uneasy. For any of us to
be at peace with the existence of hell as a reality, we must surrender it to the
hands of God knowing that he is as all just as God is all-loving. The Lord is
not looking for ways to send us to hell for our transgressions. We are left
only to choose hell for ourselves. If the Lord allows anyone to remain in hell,
it is only because he knows and loves them more than they could know or
love themselves.

Eternity lies beyond the constraints of time and space as well as history.
Our finite and limited human thought processes cannot project what happens
in eternity. My hope is that the Lord's omnipotent love will ultimately and
eventually find a way to outwit any and every human resistance found in our
free will which enables us to totally reject God and choose separation. God's
mercy is as great as God's justice, and God's justice is as great as God's love.
Thank God always that he does not choose to be separated from us. The
Apostle Paul tells us:

> "For I am convinced that neither death, nor life, nor angels, nor principalities,
> nor present things, nor future things, nor powers, nor height, nor depth, nor any
> other creature will be able to separate us from the love of God in Christ Jesus
> our Lord" (Rom. 8:38).

Final/Last Judgment

In addition to the particular judgment, which was discussed previously, there
will also be a final or last judgment. The former applies to us individually,
uniquely, and particularly and the latter applies to the consummation of the
entire world and of history itself. This final judgment determines our universal and communal destiny and is intimately connected with the Second Coming of Christ called, by its Greek name, 'The Parousia.'

Although the scriptures tell us with certainty that there will be a final or
last judgment (Matt. 25), we must place that fully in God's hands because the
scriptures also tell us many times that we should not judge others. We are
told this because, unlike God, who will be our final just judge, we would
have difficulty seeing how to really judge others with a big wooden plank
stuck in our eye (Matt. 7:3).

In the Old Testament, many of the prophets termed this final judgment,
'The Day of the Lord.'(Isa. 2:12, Ezek. 13:5). Yahweh was seen by Israel to
be the just judge of its people. The role of just judge in the New Testament is
given over to Christ as the risen Lord is seen to become the universal just
judge of all people at the last:

"I charge you in the presence of God and of Christ Jesus, who will judge the living and the dead, . . ." (2 Tim. 4:1).

In the New Testament, the final judgment often takes on an apocalyptic tone and is seen similarly to the Old Testament judgment of Sodom and Gomorrah. The Epistle 2nd Peter and the Book of Revelation make it explicitly clear that there will be a final day of judgment:

"The Lord knows how to rescue the devout from trial and to keep the unrighteous under punishment for the day of judgment . . ." (2 Pet. 2:9).

"We give thanks to you, Lord God almighty, who are and who were. For you have assumed your great power and established your reign. The nations raged, but your wrath has come, and the time for the dead to be judged, and to recompense your servants, the prophets, and the holy ones, and those who fear your name, the small and the great alike, and to destroy those who destroy the earth" (Rev. 11:17–18). And:

"Fear God and give him glory, for his time has come to sit in judgment" (Rev. 14:7).

It is not only the scriptures that tell us that there will be a final judgment as one of the last things, but also the continuous Tradition of the church. For example, in the Apostle's Creed, the Nicene Creed, and then later in the Athanasian Creed, we repeat the belief that:

"He shall come again to judge the living and the dead."

The Final Judgment is affirmed by many of the church Fathers including St Augustine: "That, therefore, which the whole Church of the true God holds and professes as its creed, that Christ shall come from heaven to judge quick and dead, this we call the last day, or last time, of the divine judgment" (Dods, *Nicene and Post-Nicene Fathers* 20:1).

The Final Judgment of God will take place in eternity, beyond the bounds of time, space, and history as we know it. To God, who lives in the present, but already knows the future, this has become a reality. At the last, this judgment will make clear three things which we already know and believe are true:

1. All of history and the historical process has been and will always be the work of a just and loving God. The outcome of history has already been decided by Christ.
2. The central point of history as well as the universe is Jesus Christ. With the birth, death, and resurrection of Jesus Christ, the universe

became once and for all, Christocentric. There will be seen to be only one coming of Christ of which the second coming or Parousia is the final stage to lay the foundation for the final judgment.

3. The moving force of the historical process was, is, and shall be the Holy Spirit-God's loving presence in the universe and in our lives.

The purpose of the general judgment is not to reconfigure one's standing before the Lord, but to reveal to everyone the full ramifications of all our good and bad deeds in relation to other people and the universe. Of course, we will know all the good and the bad we have done individually at our particular judgment, but only at the final judgment will we see what affect the way we lived our lives had on others. Only then will we truly see and understand the ultimate significance of our words and deeds. We will then be able to comprehend the kind of good or bad influence we have been, not only on those in our family or immediate circles, but also our effect on all people who may have come after us for generations and generations. We will then receive our eternal just punishment or reward.

The Scriptures mention certain signs and events which are to take place before the final judgment. These predictions were not intended to serve as indications of the exact time of the judgment, because as we are told in the scriptures, that day and hour are known only to God, the Father. They were meant to foreshadow the last judgment and to keep the end of the world ever present and utmost in the minds of Christians as the end will come when least expected like a thief in the night . . .

Theologians usually enumerate the following events as signs of the last judgment:

1. General Preaching of the Gospel

There is only one Gospel and that is the Gospel of Jesus Christ. It is seen through the eyes, mouths, and hands of Matthew, Mark, Luke, John, Paul, and other disciples who followed in their footsteps, but none the less there is only the one Gospel to proclaim to the nations. Christ speaks through the gospel writers Matthew and Mark of the preaching of the Gospel and the end of the world being tied together. The proclamation of the Gospel as a witness to all the nations is a gradual development in the gospels; but here the fulfillment of the mission to preach the Gospel is made a sign that the end is near to the Second Coming of Christ:

> "And this gospel of the kingdom will be preached throughout the world as a witness to all the nations, and then the end will come" (Matt. 24:14)(see also Matt. 28:19–20; Mark 13:10).

It is believed that the verses following this particular verse in Matthew 24:15–23 were originally written in regard to the First Jewish Revolt and the destruction of the temple. Matthew, writing after that time, knew that the Second Coming of Jesus was still in the future. Like most Christians in the early church, Matthew probably thought that the Second Coming was imminent. The Evangelist and gospel writer Matthew had probably envisioned the preaching of the Gospel to the nations and the events of those particular verses with their original intention regarding the temple as ones which foreshadowed the cosmic events and disturbances in the universe. He speaks to all of this happening prior to the second Coming of Christ. Thus, in the course of time, all the events to Matthew probably are tied together in the history of the world and belonged to what he considered to be 'the end.'

2. Conversion of the Jews

The conversion of the Jews towards the end of the world is foretold by St. Paul in the Epistle to the Romans:

> "I do not want you to be unaware of this mystery, brothers and sisters, so that you will not become wise in your own estimation: a hardening has come upon Israel in part, until the full number of the Gentiles comes in, and thus all Israel will be saved" (Rom.11:25–26).

That the conversion of the Jews would take place in the last days prior to the Second Coming was later the understanding of many of the church Fathers including St. Augustine:

> "In connection with the last judgment, the following events will come to pass as we have learned . . . the Jews will believe" (*Nicene and Post-Nicene Fathers* 20:30).

One of the scriptural sources for this belief was later taken from the prophet Hosea:

> "Then the people of Israel shall turn back and seek the Lord their God, and David their king; and they shall come trembling to the Lord and to his bounty in the last days" (Hos. 3:5).

In the 1800's, Pope Pius IX explicitly cited this particular passage as referring to the conversion of the Jews in the end times. (Pius IX, *Dives In Misericordia Deus,* February 14, 1877)

3. *Return of Enoch and Elijah*

The scriptures tell us that Elijah went up to heaven in a whirlwind and that Enoch, because he pleased God, was taken up as well and would not see death (2 Kings 2:11; Heb. 5:11). There is a belief that these two men, whose lives had never ended in death, would be reserved for the last times to be precursors of the second coming of Christ. This was a unanimous belief among the Fathers of the early church. They based this belief on several texts of Scripture (Mal. 4:5–6; Sir. 48:10; Matt. 17:11; Sir. 44:16).

4. *A Great Apostasy*

St. Paul in a letter to the Thessalonians admonishes them that they must not be terrified, as if the day of the Lord were at hand, for there must first come a revolt , the apostasy. This apocalyptic scenario used many terms which were borrowed from what was previously and prophetically written in the Old Testament apocalyptic book of Daniel (Dan. 11:36–37). This was seen by the Fathers of the church as a great falling away by Christians of many nations who depart from the faith:

> "Let no one deceive you in any way. For unless the apostasy comes first and the lawless one is revealed, the one doomed to perdition, who opposes and exalts himself above every so-called god and object of worship, so as to seat himself in the temple of God, claiming that he is a god. Do you not recall that while I was with you I told you these things" (2 Thess. 2:3–5).

5. *The Reign of the Antichrist*

In the passage mentioned above in 2 Thessalonians 2:3–5, St. Paul indicates as another sign of the day of the Lord, the revealing of the exalted so-called god, that son of perdition. "The lawless one" is generally identified with the Antichrist, who the New Testament says is to come in the last days. The word, 'Antichrist,' however, is found only in the epistles of St. John in the New Testament (1 John 2:18–22; 4:3; 2 John 7) and designates a personification of the utmost evil. The Antichrist is the prince of darkness as well as an arch enemy and deceitful impersonator of Christ. Although often seen in the broader New Testament as one mysterious adversary of Christ, the gospels seem to refer to the Antichrist as possibly a collection of deceptive persons (Matt. 24:23; Mark 13:14–22).

Christians believe that Jesus, the Messiah, will appear in his Second Coming to earth to face the emergence of the Antichrist figure, who will be the greatest false messiah ever to appear in the history of Christianity. Just as Christ is the savior of all humanity, his adversary at the end time will be a figure or figures of concentrated and unparalleled evil. Although somewhat obscure, and there are many different opinions on this subject, it is generally agreed that certain New Testament texts state that before the Parousia, the second coming, there will arise this powerful adversary of Christ who many will worship. At that time, the Antichrist will seduce the nations by his signs and wonders, and the Church will suffer tremendous persecution at the hands of the Antichrist:

> "Children, it is the last hour; and just as you heard that the antichrist was coming, so now many antichrists have appeared. Thus we know this is the last hour" (1 John 2:18).

Of the time of tribulation, the Catholic Catechism states:

> "Before Christ's second coming the Church must pass through a final trial that will shake the faith of many believers" (Cf. Luke 21:12; John 15:19–20 par. 675).

This time of trial will be marked by religious deception, apostasy from the true faith, and the rise of the antichrist. This time of trial at the end of history will reveal the fullness of antichrist:

> "a pseudo-messianism" by which man glorifies himself in place of God and of his Messiah come in the flesh. . ." (*Catechism*, 675).

History has witnessed much speculation about the antichrist, including many writings by the Church Fathers about his background and methods of destruction. What is more clear is that when history draws to a close, the Antichrist and his followers—both demonic and human—will seek to destroy as many souls as possible, unleashing diabolic destruction and causing widespread apostasy. We also know the spirit of Antichrist is already within the world, just as it has been for several thousand years.

6. Extraordinary Disturbances in Nature

The Scriptures clearly indicate that prior to the last judgment, there will be much war and several periods of famine. There will also be terrifying calamities, disturbances, and disruptions of the physical cosmos.

> "You will hear of wars and reports of wars; see that you are not alarmed for these things must happen, but it will not yet be the end. Nation will rise against nation, and kingdom against kingdom; there will be famines and earthquakes from place to place . . . Immediately after the tribulation of those days, the sun will be darkened, and the moon will not give its light, and the stars will fall from the sky, and the powers of the heavens will be shaken" (Matt. 24:6–7, 29 ; see also Mark 13:24; Luke 21:25).

Both the prophet Isaiah (700 BC) and the prophet Joel (400 BC) had prophesied prior to the gospel writers Matthew, Mark, and Luke that events similar to these disruptions in the cosmos would occur at the coming of the 'Day of the Lord.' They wrote about these universal calamities long before the above words would ever appear in the gospels (Joel 2:31; Isa. 13:10).

7. The Blazing and Burning Fire

In some of the Apostolic writings as well as in the Book of Revelation, we are told that the end of the world will be brought about through a huge, blazing, and general fire. This universal raging fire will not only transform the heavens, but will also dissolve everything in the world and burn it away. However, it will not annihilate all of the present creation, but will change it both in form and in appearance. There will be, as a result, a newly created heaven and earth:

> "But the day of the Lord will come like a thief, and then the heavens will pass away with a mighty roar and the elements will be dissolved by fire, and then the earth and everything done on it will be found out. Since everything is to be dissolved in this way, what sort of persons ought you to be, conducting yourselves in holiness and devotion, waiting for and hastening the coming of the day of God, because of which the heavens will be dissolved in flames and the elements melted by fire" (2 Pet. 3:10–12).

8. The Trumpet of Resurrection

Several texts in the New Testament make mention of a trumpeting voice or the sounding of a trumpet which will change and transform all as well as to then awaken the dead to resurrection:

> "Behold, I tell you a mystery, we shall not all fall asleep, but we will all be changed, in an instant, in the blink of an eye, at the last trumpet. For the trumpet will sound, the dead will be raised incorruptible, and we shall be changed" (1 Cor. 15:51–52). And:

> "For the Lord himself, with a word of command, with the voice of an archangel and with the trumpet of God, will come down from heaven, and the dead in Christ will rise first. Then we who are alive, who are left, will be caught up together with them in the clouds to meet the Lord in the air" (1 Thes. 4:16–17).

9. The Sign of the Son of Man Appearing in the Heavens

This is the sign immediately preceding the Second Coming of Christ, to judge the world. This sign was generally understood by the Fathers of the Church to mean the appearance in the sky of the cross on which the Lord

Jesus died or else that of a beaming cross of light; brilliant in appearance and illuminating the entire sky.

How the sign will appear in heaven, or whether it will appear in the sky above, and other details surrounding the sign, are open to debate and conjecture. What is fairly certain, however, is that the sign of Jesus Christ can only be the cross. In addition to the historical significance of the cross as the wooden structure on which Jesus died or the crucifix, the cross, in and of itself, possesses symbolic value. A symbol is more than a sign. So the cross is a mysterious symbol which in no way diminishes its historical reality as a sign.

The cross was the intersection where humanity met divinity. In speaking of the cross, the New Testament writers were most often referring symbolically to the sacrifice and redemptive work of Jesus Christ and not the literal wood of the cross (1 Cor. 1:17; Gal. 2:19, 6:14; Eph. 2:16; Phil. 3:18).

Like any symbol, its function was to first remind us of something else and then point the way to that something. A symbol should not have any definition, but many levels of meaning. Similar to a work of art, it should defy any simple description which is free of nuance. A symbol is certainly first a sign; however, it can also be distinguished from a sign by being more adequate in its aptness. The sign merely points to something else, but the symbol is closer to the reality of the thing being signified and indicates a special meaningfulness. A symbol points to and communicates the reality which lies behind it. But, because it is first a sign, it is very intimately connected with the reality that it essentially embodies and signifies. The cross as both sign and symbol is as most intimately connected to the person of Jesus of Nazareth as it will be to the Universal Christ.

In this particular sense, it is only the cross of Jesus Christ which can be considered both the personal and universal sign and the symbol of the Universal Christ. It is Jesus who makes the cross, not only his sign and symbol, but also the personal and universal sign and symbol of Christ for all generations of beings throughout all of history.

The cross is an intersection where all reality is centered in Christ. In the cross, all things are brought together and united with God (Col. 1:15–20). Through the cross, Jesus becomes the center of not only all reality and mystery, but also between God and man, eternity and history, heaven and earth, good and evil, death and life. All duality disappears at the center of the cross.

At the center of the cross is Christ, here God becomes man and man becomes God. All vertical lines of mystery in a descent from above are united with the vertical lines ascending from below. They intersect and meet with all horizontal lines of intelligible reality at the center. At that center, all duality of horizontal and vertical no longer exist; they are unified. At the center, all worldly realities; elements of earth, wind, water, and fire meet, as do all spatial directions: north, south, east, and west. All past, present, future, and eternal realities converge. Each of the four lines that make up the cross becomes a radius, and as such they radiate. As they radiate, they permeate every being in all of history and eternity. The last sign to be seen in heaven and earth, just before the Second Coming of Christ, will be the cross. How we will see it remains a mystery. But we know it will signify that Christ is now coming as judge in power and glory. The end times began with the dying and rising of Jesus, making The Second Coming and the Omega Point possible. The cross will point the way, For the Gospel tells us:

> "And then the sign of the Son of Man will appear in heaven, and the tribes of the earth will mourn, and they will see the Son of Man coming upon the clouds of heaven with power and great glory" (Matt. 24:30).

Chapter Three

Eternity and the End of Time

"Time is too slow for those who wait, too swift for those who fear, too long for those who grieve, too short for those who rejoice. But for those who love, time is not." (Henry Van Dyke, *Music and Other Poems*).

THE ANCIENTS

God's providential wisdom orders time so that day and night, months and seasons all serve a purpose in the play of life. In the Book of Genesis, in the Old Testament, the Bible begins with the words:

"In the beginning, when God . . ." (Gen. 1:1).

It suggests that at our moment in time, this the "now" moment is the only one we have at present. God was there in the beginning, in that past moment, but at this present time gives us no indication of when that was or the date or the time. We have only scientific conjecture. Similarly, and surely no accident of coincidence, the Gospel of John, in the New Testament, begins with the words:

"In the beginning was the Word, and the Word was with God, and the Word was God" (John 1:1).

God was, is, and always will be. God is in this "now" moment, but God is eternal.

Plato, one of the earliest and most famous Greek philosophers, described time as a moving image of eternity. This doesn't really tell us too much about either time or eternity, other than the fact that that they are related, there is a difference, and that eternity is truly the reality of which time is merely an image. Overall, it tells us a little about time and virtually nothing at all about eternity:

> "Wherefore he resolved to have a moving image of eternity, and when he set in order the heavens, he made this image eternal but moving according to number, while eternity itself rests in unity; and this image we call time" (*Dialogues of Plato*, Timaeus 37 c-e).

Aristotle, Plato's pupil, was a little more scientific in his approach and in theory, defines time as "a number of change in respect of the before and after." He describes time as fundamentally linked to change and movement. Time to Aristotle is derivative of motion and the "measurable aspect of motion" (Aristotle, *Physics,* Bk IV).

In his "*Confessions*, Books X to XII," the ancient philosopher and Catholic theologian, St. Augustine, the Bishop of Hippo, theologically refuted Aristotle's theory and described time as being located in the mind or soul. Past time, he maintained, is located in the memory, and future time is anticipated in the present. St Augustine also maintained that within the concept of time is the starting point and the key to attempting to understand eternity and our relationship with God, who exists outside of time:

> "For you, God, are infinite and never change . . . you yourself are eternally the same" (*Confessions,* Augustine, BK I).

MIDDLE AGES

Much later on, in the Middle Ages, one of the most influential Catholic theologians of all time and a supreme doctor of the church, St Thomas Aquinas, in a similar fashion to St. Augustine, had this to say in his *Summa* about using time as a starting point for any discussion which concerns things eternal:

> "I answer that, as we attain to the knowledge of simple things by way of compound things, so must we reach to the knowledge of eternity by means of time, which is nothing but the numbering of movement by 'before' and 'after.' For since succession occurs in every movement, and one part comes after another, the fact that we reckon before and after in movement makes us apprehend time, which is nothing else but the measure of before and after in movement. Now in a thing bereft of movement, which is always the same, there is no before or after. As therefore the idea of time consists in the numbering of before and after in movement, so likewise in the apprehension of the uniformity of what is outside of movement consists the idea of eternity. Further, those things are said to be measured by time which have a beginning and an end in time, because in everything which is moved there is a beginning, and there is an end. Whatever is wholly immutable can have no succession so it has

no beginning, and no end. Thus eternity is known from two sources: first, because what is eternal is interminable—that is, has no beginning nor end (that is, no term either way); secondly, because eternity has no succession, being simultaneously whole" (Aquinas, Part One Q 10).

In Part One Q. 10 of his *Summa*, St Thomas goes on to define eternity and time as follows:

"Eternity is the measure of permanent being, whereas time is the measure of movement." Also that, "eternity and God are the same thing."

TIME AND ETERNITY

There is an old saying, "Time is God's way of stopping everything from happening all at once." So, time is a measure in which events can be ordered from the past through the present into the future. Time is finite; God is eternal and infinite. In God there is no passage of time. There is no past, present, or future moment; God is always eternally present. However, unlike time, there is no "now" moment in eternity. It is "the now that stands, not that flows away," says St. Thomas (Aquinas, Ia, q. 10, a. 2, obj. Ia).

Eternity then, being a duration without either beginning or end, has this very distinctive characteristic, that in it there is no succession either past or future. There is only an everlasting present. There is only the entirety of eternity as one continuous and instantaneous whole.

Even our own language can get circular on us here and create some problems for us because the word, "instantaneous," circles us back to the concept of time. What this can tell us is that we can know essentially what eternity means, but we cannot picture it in our imagination. Every attempt we make to envision eternity in our imagination results merely in some lengthened view of imaginary time. The point is that time, of course, is essentially different from eternity.

EINSTEIN'S THEORY OF RELATIVITY

Einstein's *Theory of Relativity* maintains that time is relative and depends on the observer because temporal duration depends on the observer, and time as a concept can be both measured and experienced. This is true of course, but what bearing this has on the subjective concept of time would be much too lengthy to discuss as part of any treatment of time and eternity, particularly because the *Theory of Relativity* does not discuss eternity or the spiritual life at all. Therefore, we will try only to discuss known comparisons and dissimilarities between time and eternity apart from any treatment which directly concerns the *Theory of Relativity*.

SUBJECTIVE CONCEPT OF TIME

The subjective concept of time usually implies six elemental considerations, those being succession, continuity, divisibility, movement, measurability, and irreversibility. In time, the future can never be completely detached from the past and the present since it comes from the past and through the present. This connection would be impossible if the present did not come from the past and was not open to the future which is still outstanding, though not yet fully known or realized. Yesterday loses its meaning and reality if today has no tomorrow. The past is that which is gone; however, it exists because of the present which can be seen as that future which is arriving now and that future which is still outstanding. Without a future which is still outstanding there can be no concept of time as we know it.

The end of time is the human death which brings an end to all future moments in time and renders them into the immediate present. Since in death there is an end to all future moments in time, the present is always absolutely determined by this ultimate ending. Hence, for the Christian believer, the message of eternity can only be understood in light of the hope of what it says about a future which is promised in the afterlife and is progressively unveiled though not yet fully arrived. This future, even though already determined for all eternity by God, is as yet unknown to us. It can only be accepted in the mystery of the present moment as either the future gift of God in Christ or the refusal of that gift.

As Christians, we are blessed in knowing that Jesus is no stranger to our earthly life which is bound by time and mortality. He reassures us by his wounds, suffering on the cross, and risen greeting of "Peace be with you," that we will eventually rise to be with him. We are unbounded by his eternal love for us which no earthly time can weaken or destroy. As the Apostle Paul tells us in his Letter to the Romans:

> "For I am convinced that neither death, nor life, nor angels, nor principalities, nor present things, nor future things, nor powers, nor height, nor depth, nor any other creature will be able to separate us from the love of God in Christ Jesus our Lord" (Rom. 8:38–39).

In the *Encyclopedia of Theology*, edited by modern Catholic theologian, Karl Rahner, S.J., we read the following concerning the concept of time:

> "It is our faith which confesses the Providence of God by which God is not only the Lord of time, but also guarantees an ultimate meaning of time for history . . . Time is not just a determination of physical and material reality. It is also a determination of the spirit" (Rahner, "Time," 1716).

It will only be in some future moment in time as we are incorporated fully into the Godhead that all present and past moments will eventually be understood. For it would be impossible for any of us to be able to understand the beginning which took place in the past without understanding the ending of any and all present-future moments of time. This happens for each of us as we pass through our human death which leads us on into an eternity without beginning or end. In eternity we will experience time not as a limitation but as an opportunity. For us now, as death approaches, time is continually running out; in eternity, it will be continually opening up and will be endless.

CHRONOS AND KAIROS

Greek mythology depicts two very different concepts of time. The Greek language denotes two distinct principles, Chronos and Kairos. In a theological sense, Kairos is seen as qualitative as opposed to quantitative. The former refers to numeric, or chronological, time. In Greek mythology, Chronos is identified as the personification of time. He is usually portrayed as an old, wise man with a long, gray beard, much like "Father Time." The meaning of Kairos renders an altogether different concept of time. It is literally "the right or opportune moment." This relates time specifically to metaphysical or divine time. Hence, it can also be seen as "an appointed time in the purpose and plan of God." Also in the Christian sense of it, Kairos time could be perceived as "Kingdom time."

Scripture sometimes refers to Kairos time as things happening in "the fullness of times," or as "the time of fulfillment," or as at "the appointed time." For example:

> "In all wisdom and insight, he has made known to us the mystery of his will in accord with his favor that he set forth in him as a plan for the fullness of times, to sum up all things in Christ, in heaven and on earth" (Eph. 1:9–10).

> "After John had been arrested, Jesus came to Galilee proclaiming the gospel of God: 'This is the time of fulfillment. The Kingdom of God is at hand. Repent and believe in the gospel" (Mark 1:15).

Each of us will meet the end of our human life on earth at the moment of our death in the "fullness of time, at the time of fulfillment, and the appointed time," to receive our eternal retribution. The Catholic Catechism teaches us:

> "Each man receives his eternal retribution in his immortal soul at the very moment of his death, in a particular judgment that refers his life to Christ." (*Catechism* 1022).

THEOLOGY OF ETERNITY

In terms of the theological definition of eternity, the ancient definition of it was first brought forth by the Catholic lay philosopher, Boethius in the 6th century. Eternity is defined by Boethius as "possession, without succession and perfect, of interminable life" (Boethius, V, VI). This definition, which applies to eternity properly and thus applies to God, implies four things, that eternity is:

- a life,
- without beginning or end,
- without succession,
- of the most perfect kind.

By definition it implies that God not only is (essentially) or exists, but "lives." The notion of life, like all notions however abstract or spiritual, is, when applied to God, only but an analogy. As God does not live precisely as anything else with which we are familiar lives, God does not even exist as anything else exists. As Creator, God is uncreated and transcendent reality. Our notions of life, or essence and existence are derived from creatures, in which life implies change. Existence is something which is added to essence, thus it involves composition. In God there can be no composition, change, or imperfection of any kind, but all is pure act or pure being. God is "infinitely perfect" in God's eternity.

On the other hand, however, "time" involves a succession of changes and is constantly changing. Therefore for us, eternity is that condition of timeless existence beyond death which characterizes the afterlife and all that is infinite and immortal. It is, essentially, infinity without beginning or end as God is without beginning or end. Unlike events which take place in time, in eternity events do not follow a sequential pattern; they are entire or whole. One could pose the question, of course, "What was God doing before time began?" But that would be utter nonsense and an absurdity because any "before" involves time and not eternity. Even St Augustine saw this as a theological absurdity in the early centuries A.D.

God is infinite having no cause. When we call God 'infinite,' we mean that God is not limited in any way whatever. What is infinite cannot be increased or diminished but is absolutely whole, entire, and perfect. All creatures are finite or limited, and they are caused. Without an Eternal One who is Creator you cannot have creation. All created things come into existence in a point of time. While God alone is eternal in an infinite sense, God can bestow an eternal nature to a creature who had a beginning in time. This would include created beings such as angels as well as the souls of mankind.

Eternal life can be communicated to them, but it is not part of theirs or our essential nature.

The symbol of eternity is the circle without beginning or end. It is often shown in the form of a serpent eating its own tail. This is called the "Ouroboros." Another symbol which is seen to signify eternity is the mathematical symbol for infinity. In appearance, this looks like a sideways figure 8.

Infinity differs from what might be considered as a very large number for the important reason that if you subtract one from a very large number (no matter how large it is), you would have one less: on the other hand, if you subtract one from infinity, you would still have infinity.

Time stands in the same relation to eternity as a large number does to infinity. There is a sense in which infinity would include any and every large number, no matter how large, yet it is quite fundamentally different and independent of it. By analogy, eternity includes all measurements of time and yet is fundamentally something other than a measurement of an extremely long period of time. You cannot comprehend or fathom eternity as an extension of an extremely great length of time, as the only direct road which connects time and eternity for us, is that of the experience of a human life which goes through death, and then enters the afterlife. However, because they are very different categories of experiences, eternity can only be understood in the passage of life through death which for all intents and purposes is the end of time as we would know it. (Ref. see Dr. Arthur Custance, *Doorway Paper* No. 37)

Therefore, to have any complete and direct experience of eternity you must pass from the length of time which includes your human life through your death to your experience of endless eternity. God is both in time and in eternity. We can only be in one or the other to the extent that eternity includes all measurements of time but is independent of it. In his "*Joy of the Gospel,* " Pope Francis tells us that it can only be the Lord who reconciles:

> "God and man, time and eternity, flesh and spirit, person and society." (Francis I, *Joy of the Gospel*, 229)

ETERNITY NOW

Finally, there is of course, the experience of eternal life which we can have now as part of our earthly journey in time and as a foretaste of the eternal life to come. The Gospel of John tells us that eternal life for us, is not only futuristic, but also pertains to the present (John 5:24). Therefore, "eternal life" could also be seen as a term sometimes applied to the state and life of grace, even before our death, this being the initial stage of eternal life or the seed, as it were, of the never-ending life of bliss which can only flower in heaven. In this sense, grace as the gift of God, and of his Son can then be perceived, through the power of the Holy Spirit as the very first stage of eternal life. If we love passionately and are true to ourselves, to others, and to God, we will after death, pass into the second stage, the beautiful flower from the seed of life eternal here on earth. One of my favorite contemporary songs has always been *The Rose* by Bette Midler because it beautifully puts to lyrics what I am attempting to say here concerning the seed of love and the flower of eternal life.

We began this particular section on time and eternity by saying, "eternity is a circle." In the circle the beginning is the end and the end is the beginning. As we *GET TΩ THE END*, we also get to the beginning at one and the same time. God is in the present now moment both in time and in the timelessness of eternity, not only as the center of the circle, but at every point in the circle.

God is always eternal. Eternal life for us begins now. God has given us the promise of eternal life in this, the now moment before the curtain comes down to end our earthly life:

> "For God so loved the world that he gave his only Son, so that everyone who believes in him might not perish but might have eternal life . . . everyone who sees the Son and believes in him may have eternal life, and I shall raise him on the last day" (John 3:16; 6:40).

Ouroboros.

END TIMES ROLES

Cast of Characters

The Antichrist
The Communion of Saints
St. Michael
Mary, Mother of God
The Holy Spirit
God, The Father
Jesus Christ
Anonymous Christians

Chapter Four

End Times Role of the Antichrist

The Antichrist is "the villain" in the play of life. The word "antichrist" comes from the combining of two Greek words, "anti" which can be translated as *to be in place of* or *opposed to* or *against* and "Christos" which is translated as *Christ* or *the anointed one*. So, the antichrist is a false Christ who appears in the role of Christ. Christian Tradition, since the time of the Early Church Fathers came to use the name "Lucifer," meaning "Morning Star," as a proper name for Satan or the devil. Even more than being a proper name, it describes the state from which he fell. He was considered to be a beautiful angel before his fall from heaven. The Book of Isaiah in the Old Testament first describes for us the King of Babylon in chapter 14. The words will later be used by Jesus allegorically to describe Lucifer or Satan:

> "How have you fallen from the heavens O morning star, son of the dawn! How are you cut down to the ground, you who mowed down the nations! You said in your heart: 'I will scale the heavens; above the stars of God, I will set up my throne; I will take my seat on the Mount of Assembly, in the recesses of the North. I will ascend above the tops of the clouds; I will be like the most high" (Isa. 14:12–14)!

The following words were used by Jesus in the gospels to similarly describe the fall of Lucifer from heaven:

> "The seventy-two returned rejoicing, and said, 'Lord, even the demons are subject to us because of your name. Jesus said, 'I have observed Satan fall like lightening from the sky" (Luke 10:17–18).

Lucifer, Satan, Beelzebul, the devil, the beast, the dragon, and the antichrist are all names which describe the personification of evil in the bible.

The antichrist then, as the villain, is the personification of all the evil forces hostile to God. He is at one and the same time a personage who is the enemy of Christ as well as his evil-doing imitator. The idea of the antichrist arms the believing community to do battle with the forces of darkness which are personified in our own time and place in history. In the Scriptures, antichrist can either refer to people or religious systems in every generation who have the spirit of the antichrist and whose role is to work against the Holy Spirit sent by Jesus. It can also refer to a singular personage whose role at the end of times will be the personification of evil (1 John 2:18, 22; 4:3; 2 John 7).

The word antichrist itself is only found in the letters of St. John:

> "Children, it is the last hour; and just as you heard that the antichrist was coming, so now many antichrists have appeared. Thus we know that this is the last hour . . . and every spirit that does not acknowledge Jesus does not belong to God. This is the spirit of the antichrist that, as heard is to come, but in fact is already in the world . . . Many deceivers have gone out into the world, those who do not acknowledge Jesus Christ as coming in the flesh; such is the deceitful one and the antichrist" (1 John 2:18; 4:3; 2 John 1:7).

The Apostle Paul calls the antichrist, "the lawless one" and also "the one doomed to perdition:"

> "Let no one deceive you in any way. For unless the apostasy comes first and the lawless one is revealed, the one doomed to perdition, who opposes and exalts himself above every so-called god and object of worship so as to seat himself in the temple of God, claiming that he is a god- Do you not recall that while I was still with you I told you these things" (2 Thes. 2:3–5)?

The gospel writers Matthew and Mark seem to indicate that the antichrist is really a collective of persons who are false messiahs:

> "If anyone says to you then, 'Look here is the Messiah! Or, there he is! Do not believe it. False messiahs and false prophets will arise, and they will perform signs and wonders so great as to deceive, if that were possible, even the elect. Behold, I have told it to you beforehand" (Matt. 24:23NAB) (see also Mark 13:14–20).

The Book of Revelation refers to the antichrist as a collective of persons as well. It calls the antichrist, 'the beast,' 'the dragon,' 'the false prophet' and 'the devil' (see Rev. 12:3–18; 17:7–12; 20;10).

> "Then another sign appeared in the sky; it was a huge red dragon" (Rev. 12:2).

> "Then I saw a beast come out of the sea" (Rev. 13:1).

"The devil who had led them astray was thrown into the pool of fire and sulfur, where the beast and the false prophet were" (Rev. 20:10).

The most prominent name for the antichrist in the scriptures is "the beast," which is a mysterious figure with an end times role. The antichrist is referred to as "the beast" 36 times in the Book of Revelation (Rev. chapters 11–20). He will claim to be God and have tremendous religious, political, military, and economic power and authority. He will draw an audience of worshippers from all the nations of the world. The beast is identified with the number 666 in Rev. 13:18. Whereas the Book of Revelation is rich in symbolism, most theologians and biblical scholars believe that this is a play on the number 777 which is considered to be a perfect number representing wholeness or completeness. Therefore, 666 represents something short of that.

Many of the early church Fathers also wrote about the antichrist who was to come. These included Polycarp, Irenaeus, Tertullian, Hippolytus, Origen, Jerome, and Augustine. In fact, by the time of St. Irenaeus in the third century, it was widely taught that the antichrist would be a human figure, a person, who would rule the world on behalf of Satan, for a brief period at the end of history as we know it. His reign would be brought to an end by the intervention of the Lord himself at his Second Coming.

In the Tradition of the church, the Catholic Catechism outlines a continuous belief in the antichrist to come at the end of time:

"Before Christ's second coming, the Church must pass through a final trial that will shake the faith of many believers. The persecution that accompanies her pilgrimage on earth will unveil the "mystery of iniquity" in the form of a religious deception offering men an apparent solution to their problems at the price of apostasy from the truth. The supreme religious deception is that of the Antichrist, a pseudo-messianism by which man glorifies himself in place of God and of his Messiah come in the flesh" (*Catechism* 675).

"The Antichrist's deception already begins to take shape in the world every time the claim is made to realize within history that messianic hope which can only be realized beyond history through the eschatological judgment. The Church has rejected even modified forms of this falsification of the kingdom to come under the name of millenarianism, especially the 'intrinsically perverse' political form of a secular messianism" (*Catechism* 676).

The idea of the antichrist springs from many of the Jewish writers prior to the age of Christianity who described the Messiah as having to appear at the end of history, not only to renew all things, but to participate in a mighty cosmic struggle between good and evil. The battle would take place against a mysterious and formidable evil adversary. The primary source of this thought appears to have come from the Books of Daniel and Ezekiel in the Old

Testament. Much of the New Testament Book of Revelation in addressing the coming of the antichrist is rooted in these apocalyptic books.

In addition to the role of the antichrist in the last days prior to the Second Coming of Christ, there is much mention of "stand ins," in the play of life; false prophets, false apostles, and false teachers who arise and would be puppets of the antichrist. They would falsely claim the gift of divine inspiration or prophetic utterance and use that gift for evil ends. The rising of false prophets, apostles, and teachers in the last days is discussed throughout the New Testament (i.e., Matt. 24:11, 24; Mark 13:22; Luke 6:26; 2 Pet. 2:1, 3:3; 1 John 4:1, 4; 2 Cor. 11:13; Gal. 2:4; Jude 1:17–18; Rev. 16:13; 19:20; 20:10).

Paul relates to us that Satan is already at work in the world, however, the antichrist cannot appear as yet because someone or something is holding him back and preventing his appearance. When he does appear it will usher in the Second Coming of Christ to destroy him.

> "And now you know what is restraining, that he may be revealed in his time. For the mystery of lawlessness is already at work. But the one who restrains is to do so only for the present, until he is removed from the scene. And then the lawless one will be revealed, whom the Lord Jesus will kill with the breath of his mouth and render powerless by the manifestation of his coming" (2 Thes. 2:6–8).

Finally, we must address that which assists the pure personification of evil and a pure demonic figure which will be found in the antichrist at the end of times. We can term this, "anonymous power." This is an insidious force of evil found in the societies of the world. It is the power of changing moods, current fashion, the forces of ignorance and cynicism, and what Pope Francis has called 'the globalization of indifference,' especially the indifference to grinding poverty, hunger, and homelessness. We often serve this "anonymous power" without seeing the face of evil behind it. In the Gospels, we see it at work in the crowd which unknowingly and unwittingly serves "anonymous power." As the chorus had done in the dramatic plays of ancient times, the people collectively cry out:

> "Take him away! Crucify him" (John 19:15).

The best way for any of us to guard against being misled by any of these antichrists, false prophets, false teachers, and being among those who unwittingly serve the force of anonymous power, is to know the truth by staying in what is called the 'Hermeneutic Circle.' This can be seen as a three legged stool consisting of the reading and study of sacred Scripture as an entire whole, while subjecting oneself to the authority of the Tradition of the church and what it teaches; then intermingling both of those with our own personal/ communal faith and conscience.

Chapter Five

End Times Role of the Communion of Saints

"The Saints on earth, and those above,
But one communion make;
Joined to their Lord in bonds of love,
All of His grace partake." (John Wesley)

WHAT IS THE COMMUNION OF SAINTS?

We all have a role in the play of life. But, God does not want to save us as individuals. We do not speak of the saints, those above and those on earth as individuals in their sanctity, but as a communion. The Communion of Saints is the church throughout time and on into eternity. It includes all members of the Christian church, both living and dead, in spiritual union with one another and with God. It includes those on earth, in heaven, and in an intermediate state. We participate in the same mystical body with Christ as the head. All have been transformed by the grace of Christ. The dogma is rooted in the Scriptures and is confirmed by the Tradition of the church:

"As a body is one though it has many parts, and all of the parts of the body, though many, are one body, so also is Christ" (1 Cor. 12:12).

And in the Apostles Creed we pray:

"I believe . . .in the Holy Catholic Church, the Communion of Saints . . . "

THE ROLE OF THE COMMUNION OF SAINTS

The communion of the saints refers to believers throughout history; believers in the past, believers in the present, and believers in the years to come unto the end of time, sharing a common salvation in our Savior, the Lord Jesus Christ. Those who have passed from this world into the presence of Christ at the death of their body have the same salvation as believers who are alive today. Those who will come after us in the future will have the same promise of salvation we have.

The Communion of Saints' describes the fellowship or tie which unites Christians together, one with another, for if all Saints, living or dead, have communion with God, it follows that all have communion one with another, in Him, across the boundaries of time and space. As a communion, we are bound together by Christ's love as well as a supernatural chain of faith and hope. It is our role in the Communion of Saints to be at present a symphony of being until we enter into full communion with souls of the future who are at present known only to God.

There is something special about the word, 'communion,' for Catholics. What probably comes to mind is Holy Communion, our sharing in the Body and Blood of Christ at Mass. In this marvelous and mystical communion, we all play our part. We all matter to each other because we matter to the Lord who alone can make us saints.

At the present time we know that the church here on earth is very far from being perfect. We don't have to look much beyond our own mirror to know this. If we believe we are perfect then we should get a second opinion. For the time being, we must accept the fact that we are at best, "imperfect saints." The inter-communion of holy and unholy in the church is exactly in accordance with the predictions of Jesus Christ himself, for while He often spoke of the power of God's grace to change and sanctify the hearts of the disciples of "The Kingdom of Heaven," he also expressly foretold that there would be weeds in his field along with the wheat. Jesus said further that the Gospel net would catch bad fish as well as good fish. Both should be retained in the net until the angels make the separation at the end of time (Matt. 13:47–50):

> "He proposed another parable to them: 'The Kingdom of Heaven may be likened to a man who sowed good seed in his field. While everyone was asleep his enemy came and sowed weeds all through the wheat, and then went off. When the crop grew and bore fruit, the weeds appeared as well . . . Let them grow together until harvest; then at harvest time I will say to the harvesters, 'First collect the weeds and tie them in bundles for burning; but gather the wheat into my barn'" (Matt. 13:24–26, 30).

Throughout the New Testament, those whom Saint Paul addresses in his letters as "saints," are rebuked for almost every kind of sin imaginable. Both of his letters to the Corinthians depict many rebukes for things like schism, fornication, worship of idols, corruption of spiritual gifts, profane worship of God, heresy as well as misbelief. In his letter to the Ephesians, while St Paul affirms those who had made great advances in the understanding of the mysteries of the faith, he also rebukes them and warns them to abstain from lying, violent anger, stealing, foul speaking, bitterness, malice, and much unkindness (Eph. 4:25–32). This should tell us that we should paint with a broad brush while giving a very wide meaning with the words "Communion of Saints."

The word 'Catholic' means 'universal.' Catholics often refer to the celebration of the Eucharist as both "The Lord's Supper" and "Holy Communion." Here we celebrate the bond of union we have with the Lord and with one another in the Communion of Saints both in this world and the next:

> "While they were eating, Jesus took bread, said the blessing, broke it and giving it to his disciples said, 'Take and eat; this is my body.' Then he took a cup, gave thanks, and gave it to them, saying, 'Drink from it, all of you, for this is my blood of the covenant which will be shed on behalf of many for the forgiveness of sins'" (Matt. 26:26–28).

St Paul in his New Testament letters would appeal to all followers of Christ both in his time as well as in all generations following, to come together to remember and celebrate the bond of union we have with God and with one another. This bond of union, ordained by the Lord himself, empowers us to maintain communion both outwardly and visibly, as well as inwardly and spiritually as we celebrate the one body within the entire Communion of Saints:

> "The cup of blessing that we bless, is it not a participation in the blood of Christ? The bread that we break, is it not a participation in the body of Christ? Because the loaf of bread is one, we, though many, are one body, for we all partake of the one loaf" (1 Cor. 10:16–17).

The gospel proclaims that the road to joining the Communion of Saints in heaven is the way of Jesus Christ, crucified and risen. The role we play entails being loving, faith-filled, poor in spirit, kind and merciful, pure of heart, a peacemaker, and hungry for righteousness; furthermore, to be other-centered rather than self-centered. It is the role of every saint within the communion to follow the original script and then to pray for one another. While we pray for others near and far, others in this world and the next have been and are still praying for us. Near and far, we are all One in Christ who reminds us that our "God is a God of the living and not of the dead" (Mark 12:27,).

We should be praying and begging daily for the intercession of the saints. Here on earth, our role is to intercede for them while they are interceding for us. The letter to the Hebrews tells us:

> "Therefore, since we are surrounded by so great a cloud of witnesses, let us rid ourselves of every burden and sin that clings to us and persevere in running the race that lies before us while keeping our eyes fixed on Jesus, the leader and perfecter of faith" (Heb. 12:1–2).

Pope John Paul II has said:

> "The church brought Christ the key to understanding that great and fundamental reality that is man. For man cannot be fully understood without Christ. Or man is incapable of understanding himself fully without Christ. He cannot understand who he is, nor what his true dignity is, nor what his vocation is, nor what his final end is. He cannot understand any of this without Christ" (John Paul II, *To Set Fire on Earth*).

As we move in the direction of the Omega Point of the history of this world, we do so knowing that following our own trials and tribulations here, our death, the Second Coming of Christ, and the judgment of God, we prayerfully and hopefully anticipate full communion with all the saints of God. In the meantime, the entire chorus of saints throughout the universe will continue to sing as one in harmony:

> "When the saints go marching in, oh when the saints go marching in; I want to be in that number, when the saints go marching in!"

Chapter Six

End Times Role of St. Michael

MICHAEL, THE NAME

St. Michael is a hero in this play of life. The name, "Michael," is derived from the ancient Hebrew name (Mikha'el). In ancient times, personal names were intended to reveal one's character. Unlike our language, in the Hebrew language, the name held important significance in personalizing the identity of the individual. With this in mind, the manner in which the ancient Hebrews translated the name, "Michael," certainly fits the character. It is translated to mean, "Who is like God?" Note the question mark, because the connotation is not a statement, it is a question. If it were a statement, the meaning of the name would certainly be rendered differently. Many books on the etymology of names today make the error of translating the name as if it made the statement, "Who is like God." And that, of course, was Satan's claim before God and why he fell from heaven; he wanted to be Godlike. The Church Fathers gave Satan the name Lucifer. We find Satan's refrain in the Book of Isaiah:

"I will be like the Most High" (Isa. 14:14).

MICHAEL, THE ARCHANGEL

Michael is considered an archangel in the Jewish, Christian, and Islamic Traditions. An archangel is considered to be an angel of the highest rank. An angel, (angelus), is a messenger and is a spiritual being, intermediate between God and man. Michael is one of seven archangels in the Hebrew Tradition and has historically been referred to as "the prince of the heavenly host," "the viceroy of heaven," "the prince of light," and "the guardian of paradise." Michael is often depicted in art wielding a sword or a spear. His name (Who is like God?) was the war-cry of the good angels in heaven who fought against the evil angels at the beginning of time.

His name is referenced four times in scripture. First, in the Old Testament apocalyptic Book of Daniel, the angel Gabriel says to Daniel when he asks God to permit the Jews to return to Jerusalem:

"The prince of the kingdom of Persia stood in my way for twenty-one days, until finally Michael, one of your chief princes, came to help me . . . No one supports me against all these but Michael, your prince" (Dan. 10:13, 22).

Then in Daniel, chapter 12, the angel is speaking about the last days and the end of the world as well as the Antichrist as he says:

> "At that time there shall arise Michael, the great prince, guardian of your
> people. It shall be a time unsurpassed in distress since nations began until that
> time. At that time your people shall escape, everyone who is found written in
> the book. Many of those who sleep in the dust of the earth shall awake; some
> shall live forever, others shall be an everlasting horror and disgrace" (Dan.
> 12:1–2).

The Old Testament Book of Daniel is the only specific reference to the archangel Michael by name in the entire Old Testament. However, there are several other veiled references to him. In the New Testament, the first reference to him is in the Epistle of Jude where an allusion is made concerning a dispute between the archangel Michael and Satan over the body of Moses. Moses' death and burial is referenced in Deuteronomy where it says regarding Moses:

> "To this day, no one knows the place of Moses burial" (Deut. 34:6).

What the verse in the Epistle of Jude seems to be referring to is a discussion between the archangel Michael and Satan outlined in the apocryphal book, *The Assumption of Moses.* This was confirmed early on by the church Father Origen. (Brown et al. *Principiis III*.2.2) Here, God dispatches Michael to bury the body of Moses which Satan wants to lay claim to on the grounds of its materiality:

> "Yet the archangel Michael, when he argued with the devil in a dispute over
> the body of Moses, did not venture to pronounce a reviling judgment upon him
> but said, 'May the Lord rebuke you'" (Jude 1:9).

The final reference to the archangel Michael is in the Book of Revelation which is a book speaking to us of the end times and the Second Coming of Christ. It does focus in a veiled way on the events of the time it was written; however, it also speaks to us prophetically of the new heaven and new earth which will be inaugurated at the end of time and history. The archangel Michael is mentioned specifically by name in chapter 12. Here it depicts Satan as the accuser of God's people and Michael as the defender.

As was described at the beginning of this book, the evangelist, John, is said to have written the Book of Revelation in a cave on the Greek island of Patmos. Here he is speaking about the great battle which is to take place at the end of time which is a mirror of the battle which took place at the beginning of time. The Messiah's exaltation is inextricably linked with Michael's victory made possible by the enthronement of the lamb. The victory doesn't belong to Michael as it is God's victory. Michael is God's prince and God's supreme archangel, but he is first and foremost, God's servant. The evangelist John tells us:

> "Then war broke out in heaven; Michael and his angels battled against the dragon. The dragon and its angels fought back, but they did not prevail and there was no longer any place for them in heaven. The huge dragon, the ancient serpent, who is called the devil and Satan, who deceived the whole world, was thrown down to earth, and its angels were thrown down with it. Then I heard a loud voice in heaven say: 'Now have salvation and power come, and the Kingdom of our God and the authority of his Anointed for the accuser of our brothers is cast out, who accuses them before our God day and night. They conquered him by the blood of the lamb and by the word of their testimony; . . ." (Rev. 12:7–11).

In addition to scriptural sources, the end times role of St. Michael is also mentioned in many of the Judeo-Christian apocryphal books, such as *The Book of Enoch, The Assumption of Moses, The War of the Sons of Light against the Sons of Darkness, The Shepard of Hermas, The Revelation of Moses, and the Dead Sea Scrolls* in which the reader is told:

> "this was written for a remote generation yet to come." (*Dead Sea Scrolls, Book of Enoch* 1)

Many of the early Church Fathers also discuss St. Michael's end times role. These include many of the Greek Fathers as well as Ireneus, Tertullian, Origen, Basil the Great, Bellarmine, Bonaventure, Pseudo-Dionysius. In the middle ages, St Thomas Aquinas refers to Michael as "the Prince of the Angels" (Aquinas Ia. 113.3).

Up until recent times, Catholics recited a prayer to St. Michael which was said at the end of each Mass. It was composed by Pope Leo XIII in 1884 following a vision he had of St. Michael battling against the devil and his angels:

> "Saint Michael the Archangel, defend us in battle; be our protection against the wickedness and snares of the devil. May God rebuke him, we humbly pray:

and do thou, O Prince of the Heavenly Host, by the power of God, cast into hell Satan and all evil spirits who wander through the world seeking the ruin of souls. Amen" (Leo XIII, "Prayer to St. Michael").

In art, St. Michael's role is often depicted as being an angelic warrior, fully armed with helmet, sword, and shield, as he overcomes Satan, represented as a dragon and sometimes as a man-like figure. The shield often bears the inscription: "Quis ut Deus," the translation of the archangel's name in Latin, "Who is like God?" This is also capable of being seen as St. Michael's rhetorical and scornful question to Satan. The Scapular of St. Michael the Archangel also bears this particular phrase.

THE ROLE OF ST. MICHAEL

As the heroic leader of God's angels and archangels, Christian Tradition gives to St. Michael these particular end times roles:

1. Fight against Satan until the end of time
2. Rescue the souls of the faithful from the powers of the enemies of God
3. Be a champion of all God's people; Jews under the Old Covenant and Christians under the New Covenant
4. At the time of death, to accompany the dead into the presence of God for judgment.

The final end times role of St. Michael is indicated to be escorting the dead into the presence of God for judgment. It will then be Michael's role and mission at the end of time to champion the Jewish people as he has always done historically under the Old Covenant. He will continue to be their guardian just as he has been for the body of Moses. In fact, Moses could even be a symbol or metaphor for the entire Jewish people throughout history.

Finally, because of the sacrifice of the Lamb of God outlined in the New Testament, particularly in the Book of Revelation, St. Michael's role will be to act as the heroic champion for all Christians who have died as well. At the end of time, he will then enthrone, exalt, and serve Jesus Christ along with all Christians throughout time. This has been promised and foretold under the New Covenant. Michael, the archangel will be empowered by God to win God's victory. Then all God's people will be able to say in unison along with Michael, 'Who is like God?'

Chapter Seven

End Times Role of the Mother of God

The Holy Spirit chose Mary to be the "Leading Lady" and her "yes" to God was her very first act as a hero in the play of life. She is our star, Stella Maris; Star of the Sea.

MARY'S ROLE AT THE END

"Hail Mary, full of grace . . . Holy Mary, Mother of God, pray for us sinners now and at the hour of our death. Amen."

The above lines from the Christian prayer devoted to Mary are rooted in Luke's Gospel (Luke 1:26–28). The Hail Mary prayer has been part of the Tradition of the church in some form since the year 1050. It was made a part of the profession of faith and placed in the Council of Trent catechism in 1545. The prayer indicates that when we die, at the very end, Mary will be there praying for us. Whether the first coming or second coming of Christ, she will always be inextricably linked to her son, Jesus. Therefore, she will play a key role in the coming of the Kingdom of God in all its fullness. She has and will continue to crush the head of the antichrist for all time.

Since Mary is Jesus' mother, it must be concluded that she is also the Mother of God: If Mary is the mother of Jesus, and if Jesus is God, then Mary is the Mother of God. Mary's role in the Church is inseparable from her union with Christ and flows directly from it. Therefore she is also considered to be our mother given at the foot of the cross by our Lord and Savior, Jesus Christ; first to the Apostle John, and subsequently to us as followers of Christ. The Catechism of the Catholic Church tells us:

"Finally, the Immaculate Virgin, preserved free from all stain of original sin, when the course of her earthly life was finished, was taken up body and soul into heavenly glory, and exalted by the Lord as Queen over all things, so that she might be the more fully conformed to her Son, the Lord of lords and conqueror of sin and death. The Assumption of the Blessed Virgin is a singular participation in her Son's Resurrection and an anticipation of the resurrection of other Christians: She is our Mother in the order of grace. This motherhood of Mary in the order of grace continues uninterruptedly from the consent which she loyally gave at the Annunciation and which she sustained without wavering beneath the cross, until the eternal fulfillment of all the elect" (*Catechism* 966–969).

There are four dogmas stating important aspects of Mary's end times role in salvation and her personal relationship with God. They are:

- Divine Motherhood
- Perpetual Virginity
- Immaculate Conception
- Assumption

Mary is considered as an eschatological (last things) icon of all the followers of Christ. In her we contemplate what the Christian Church already is in her mystery and what she will be in heaven at the end of her journey. You cannot separate Mary from Jesus and you cannot separate Mary from the church. Her role will be a key one until the end of time. *The Dogmatic Constitution on the Church* from Vatican II had this to say regarding Mary's role:

"By reason of the gift and role of divine maternity, by which she is united with her Son, the Redeemer, and with His singular graces and functions, the Blessed Virgin is also intimately united with the Church" (Vatican Council II, Ch. VIII).

Although Mary is mentioned by name in the gospels and the book of Acts, she is hardly referred to at all in the entire body of Paul's New Testament letters. There is a vague reference to a woman in chapter 12 of the Book of Revelation written by the apostle John. It is believed that Mary can be seen as a prefigure and model of this woman; however, the reference to the woman is most likely applied to God's people in the Old and New Testaments at the Second Coming of Christ:

"A great sign appeared in the sky, a woman clothed with the sun, with the moon under her feet, and on her head a crown of twelve stars. She was with child and wailed aloud in pain as she labored to give birth. Then another sign appeared in the sky; it was a huge red dragon, with seven heads and ten horns, and on its heads were seven diadems. Its tail swept away a third of the stars in the sky and hurled them down to earth. Then the dragon stood before the woman about to give birth, to devour her child when she gave birth. She gave birth to a son, a male child, destined to rule all the nations with an iron rod. Her child was caught up to God and to his throne. The woman herself fled into the desert where she had a place prepared by God, that there she might be taken care of for twelve hundred and sixty days . . . When the dragon saw that it had been thrown down to earth, it pursued the woman who had given birth to the male child. But the woman was given the two wings of a great eagle, so she could fly to her place in the desert . . . The dragon became angry with the woman and went off to wage war against the rest of her offspring, those who keep God's commandments and bear witness to Jesus" (Rev. 12:1–6; 13–14; 17–18).

MARY, THE END TIME FULFILLMENT OF THE CHURCH

At the Second Vatican Council in 1964, Mary's role at the end of time was depicted in the Council Document, *Dogmatic Constitution on the Church/ Lumen Gentium* on several occasions. Much of what was stated there was confirmed later in the papal encyclical *Redemptoris Mater* in 1987. Mary, Mother of God, is to be for us the model of the church as we move toward the end of days:

"As St Ambrose taught, the Mother of God is a type of the Church in the order of faith, charity, and the perfect union with Christ" (Vatican Council II, *Lumen Gentium* 63).

"The Mother of God is already the eschatological fulfilment of the Church: "In the most holy Virgin the Church has already reached that perfection whereby she exists without spot or wrinkle" (cf. Eph. 5:27). At the same time the Council says that 'the followers of Christ still strive to increase in holiness by conquering sin, and so they raise their eyes to Mary, who shines forth to the whole community of the elect as a model of the virtues" (Vatican Council II, *Lumen Gentium* 65).

"In this eschatological fulfilment, Mary does not cease to be the "Star of the Sea" (Maris Stella) for all those who are still on the journey of faith. 'Taken up to heaven, she did not lay aside this saving role, but by her manifold acts of intercession, continues to win for us gifts of eternal salvation.' Mary contributes in a special way to the union of the pilgrim church on earth with the eschatological and heavenly reality of the Communion of Saints, since she has already been 'assumed into heaven.' The glory of serving does not cease to be her royal exaltation: assumed into heaven, she does not cease her saving service, which expresses her maternal mediation until the eternal fulfillment of all the elect" (Vatican Council II, *Lumen Gentium* 62).

"Connected with this exaltation of the noble 'Daughter of Sion' through her Assumption into heaven is the mystery of her eternal glory. For the Mother of Christ is glorified as 'Queen of the Universe'" (Vatican Council II, *Lumen Gentium* 55, 59).

"In the interim just as the Mother of Jesus, glorified in body and soul in heaven, is the image and beginning of the Church as it is to be perfected is the world to come, so too does she shine forth on earth, until the day of the Lord shall come, as a sign of sure hope and solace to the people of God during its sojourn on earth" (Vatican Council II, *Lumen Gentium* 68).

"The entire body of the faithful pours forth instant supplications to the Mother of God and Mother of men that she, who aided the beginnings of the Church by her prayers, may now, exalted as she is above all the angels and saints, intercede before her Son in the fellowship of all the saints, until all families of people, whether they are honored with the title of Christian or whether they still do not know the Saviour, may be happily gathered together in peace and harmony into one people of God" (Vatican Council II, *Lumen Gentium* 69).

"Being through, with, and for her Son on earth, it would seem fitting for Mary to be through, with, and for her Son in heaven, too. She was on earth the generous associate of her Son. The Assumption tells us that this association continues in heaven. Mary is indissolubly linked to her Son on earth and in heaven" (Vatican Council II, *Lumen Gentium* 61, 56).

"Glorified in body and soul, Mary is already in the state that will be ours after the resurrection of the dead at the end of time. The Assumption of Mary is a promise of immortality for all human beings as followers of Christ. The Assumption highlights the unity of body and soul, their respective dignity and fulfillment. In the Kingdom of Heaven, Mary's active involvement in salvation history is not finished and it continues: "Taken up to heaven, she did not lay aside her salvific duty . . . By her maternal love she cares for the brothers and sisters of her Son who still journey on earth." Mary is the 'eschatological icon of the Church'" (*Catechism* 972).

Mary, as an icon of the church, was, is, and always will be the Mother of God. She was chosen by God and destined to be the first church in her role as the *Theotokos,* the God-bearer. This also means that she will be present as a model of the last church. As was stated above, "Mary is the eschatological icon of the church" (*Catechism* 972). She is a preeminent and highly exalted member of the Communion of Saints by reason of her unique relationship with Christ. Our unity with her as church is an expression of our unity with Christ. This implies that as the Communion of Saints looks forward to the Second Coming of Christ, the church must continually be contemplating in Mary her own role at the "end of times."

END TIMES ROLE OF THE TRIUNE GOD

"Glory to the Father, and to the Son, and to the Holy Spirit, as it was in the beginning, is now, and will be forever. Amen. Alleluia!"
—*Trinitarian doxology*

Chapter Eight

End Times Role of the Holy Spirit

THE THIRD PERSON OF THE TRINITY

The Holy Spirit is "the Director" of the play of life. As Christians, we believe in the absolute mystery of the Trinity; Father, Son, and Holy Spirit as Triune God. Although this mystery has been revealed to us, we cannot fully understand it; it can only be expressed in terms of analogy. The mystery of the Trinity transcends our human imagination and even if we think we understand it, we don't. When we express the mystery of the Trinity by analogy, we can't depict it exactly. For example, the Trinity can be compared to water which can exist as water, ice, or steam; the dissimilarities will always outweigh the similarities of the analogy. This is because the Trinity is a transcendent reality which we are comparing to a human reality.

One of the things we can say of our belief in a Triune God, however, is what we recite together in both the Apostles Creed and the Nicene Creed: "We believe in the Holy Spirit."

If we believe in a Triune God as one God in three persons, then we also believe that the Father is wholly in the Son and the Holy Spirit; the Holy Spirit is wholly in the Father and the Son. We can experience the Holy Spirit within us sent by the Father and/through the Son as it proceeds. In the mystery of the Trinity, therefore, God calls us to intimate union with the Father and the Son through the Holy Spirit. They cannot be separated as they are One God in three persons; they are one nature, connatural and consubstantial. That being the case, if we are in union with the Father and Son and/through the Holy Spirit at our time and place in the procession of history; then we are living, "in the Spirit," between the already and the not yet of the Kingdom of God. We should also realize then that we are not the sole depository of the Holy Spirit, the entire church is, as the sacrament of the

Kingdom of God. You cannot separate the procession of the Holy Spirit to the end of history from the church. The term, "Holy," itself applies to anyone or anything which is consecrated to God. It is the role of the Holy Spirit within the consecrated people of God as, "temples of the Holy Spirit," to continue to transform lives until the Second Coming of Christ at the Parousia. Where God's Spirit is, there is the church until the end of time:

> "Do you not know that you are the temple of God, and that the Spirit of God dwells in you? If anyone destroys God's temple, God will destroy that person; for the temple of God, which you are, is holy" (1 Cor. 3:16–17).

"So then you are no longer strangers and sojourners, but you are fellow citizens with the holy ones and members of the household of God, built upon the foundation of the apostles and prophets, with Christ Jesus himself as the capstone. Through him the whole structure is held together and grows into a temple sacred in the Lord; in him you also are being built together into a dwelling place of God in the Spirit" (Eph. 2:19–22).

THE DYNAMISM OF THE HOLY SPIRIT

The role of the Holy Spirit as the Director in the play is to always be guiding us (John 16:13), and also continuously baptizing (Matt. 3:11), revealing (Luke 2:26), reconciling (Eph. 2:16–18), renewing (Tit. 3:5), cleansing (John 13:1–20), purifying (2 Cor. 6:14–18), unifying (1 Cor. 12:12–31), loving (Eph. 5:22), healing (1 Cor. 12:9), inspiring (Luke 2:27), transforming (2 Cor. 3:18), empowering (1 Cor. 5:4–5), saving (1 Cor. 5:5), teaching (John 14:15–31), interceding (Rom. 8:26–27), rebuking (Luke 9:42), sanctifying (Eph. 5:21–33), and drawing the people of God into a closer relationship with Jesus Christ and with one another (1 Cor. 12:1–30). In doing all this, it is also the continuing role of the Holy Spirit to bring out the best in those who will bear the fruit of the Spirit for the coming Kingdom of God:

> "The fruit of the Spirit is love, joy, peace, patience, kindness, generosity, faithfulness, gentleness, and self-control" (Gal. 5:22–23).

These are called "fruit," in the singular, and not "fruits," in the plural, because they all flow from love.

The Catholic Catechism tells us more about the missionary role of the Holy Spirit in proceeding with us and in us unto the end of history:

> " By his coming, which never ceases, the Holy Spirit causes the world to enter into the 'last days,' the time of the church, the Kingdom already inherited though not yet consummated" (*Catechism* 732).

"The Holy Spirit is in the leading role, as 'the principal agent of the whole of the Church's mission.' It is he who leads the Church on her missionary paths. This mission continues and in the course of history, unfolds the mission of Christ, who was sent to evangelize the poor; so the Church urged on by the Spirit of Christ, must walk the road Christ himself walked, a way of poverty and obedience, of service and self-sacrifice, even to death, a death from which he emerged victorious by his resurrection. So it is that the blood of the martyrs is the seed of Christians" (*Catechism* 852).

It is in the Gospel of John in particular, that we find the nature of the Holy Spirit more in evidence. Christ promises in his farewell discourse that he will send "another comforter" who will represent him in his absence and that the Holy Spirit will remain with the disciples to finish the work begun by the Father and Jesus. We are told that his work will continue until the end of time (John 14:16, 25). The Spirit would also give testimony to Jesus Christ and teach and explain his work and mission (1 John 2:1).

Finally, the Holy Spirit would work within the church unto the end of the age as the principle of life to produce within disciples the love, character, virtue, and inner life of Christ for all the world to see. And it will be the Holy Spirit, who as our advocate, will direct and guide the followers of Christ to all truth and declare what is to come (John 16:13). Ultimately, it will be the role of the Holy Spirit to be for us the pledge of our own resurrection at the end of time:

"If the Spirit of the one who raised Jesus from the dead dwells in you, the one who raised Christ from the dead will give life to your mortal bodies also, through his Spirit that dwells in you" (Rom. 8:11).

Chapter Nine

Providence, the Design of the End

THE ONGOING AND END TIMES ROLE OF GOD, THE FATHER

God, the Father, is "the Producer" of the play of life. Divine Providence is one of the many names we have for God. Providence implies that God, the Father, is not only the Lord of time, but also the Lord of all history and its ultimate meaning. It is through *Provide*-nce, that God *provide*-s for us.

If we consider the world around us and all that God has created . . . heaven and earth and the beautiful order within this vast universe which reigns . . . it manifests an infinite and almighty power behind it all. It could only be created in love, wisdom and goodness. When we look at all this, we can only be awed and begin to proclaim along with the resounding chorus of the Communion of Saints, throughout the universe "How Great Thou Art."

God is not only eternal and infinite; God is omniscient, thoroughly understands his creation, and governs it with Fatherly love, wisdom, and purpose. Providence, can be seen as a sort of extension of God's wisdom:

> "Indeed, she reaches from end to end mightily and governs all things well . . .
> But your Providence, O Father! Guides it . . ." (Wisd. 8:1; 14:3).

So, God's divine plan for any of us as creatures to attain our purpose is called God's Providence. Things are called "providential" when they make provision for the future, as the root meaning of the word *Providence* comes from the Latin *pro-videre* which means *to see ahead*. Only God has seen to the end of times and knows now what our destiny and end will be.

ST THOMAS AND PROVIDENCE

St. Thomas Aquinas, in his *Summa* had this to say concerning Divine Providence, God's governing of the universe, and the ordering of all things toward their end:

> "Since God is the cause of all things by His intellect (in conjunction with His will), it is necessary that the type of the order of things toward their end should pre-exist in the divine mind; and the type of things ordered toward an end is, properly speaking, providence" (Aquinas, Ia, q. 22, a. 1).

Because the greater does not come from the less; the more perfect does not come from the less perfect. St. Thomas maintained that this gave evidence that there was a "Prime Mover" behind all of it and ordering all things toward their end in the universe. He saw the Divine Providence of God at work in producing the order which prevails in the universe. The fact is this, that in nature, in those things that lack intelligence, we have an admirable ordering of means to ends which produces what is best. Says St. Thomas:

> "This is evident, since those things which lack intelligence—the heavenly bodies, plants and animals—act always, or at least nearly always, in such a way as to produce what is best" (Aquinas, Ia, q. 2, a. 3).

Providence Orders and Governs

In a theological sense then, Providence refers to The Father's divine plan in ordering and shaping the universe, history, and every human being within history . . . past, present, and future, throughout time as we know it. In God's wisdom, He so orders all events within the universe that the end designed for each human being he created in history may be realized at the end of history as we know it. God governs the affairs of men and works through the natural order of things so that all creation and created beings are then ordered by God to a definite end which does not negate our free will in any way, but works in conjunction with it to produce what is best.

Providence and Free Will

Providence itself is in God, of God, and one with God's essence. As creatures, we do participate with The Father in designing our own end in cooperation with Providence by virtue of our free acts and choices. God provides his loving care and grace-filled guidance for our individual lives and we choose through attempting to discern his will for us and then following it or not. Our end and ultimate destiny will depend on Divine Providence, but only after the choices we've made during our lifetime. God knows already what our choices will have been throughout our lifetime. So, God accomplishes his will through secondary causes such as the laws of nature and our human choices. In other words, through Divine Providence, The Father usually works indirectly to intervene benevolently in the affairs of humankind to accomplish the will of God.

Without freedom, we would not be human and could not even will to love God or love others in return. We also would not have the ability inherent in our will to mold our character or shape our destiny in cooperation with grace and the Providence of God. On the other hand, it is also freedom which gives us the ability granted by God to separate ourselves from God and from others. Unless we are really free, we cannot be justly held responsible for our actions. St Thomas has said in his *Summa*:

> "The proper act of free-will is choice: for we say that we have a free-will because we can take one thing while refusing another, and this is to choose" (Aquinas, Part I, Q. 83, Art. III).

While Providence guides and governs to produce what is best, free will makes choices. God in his omniscience has foreknowledge of every choice we will ever make both now and in the future. His Providence has already taken those choices into account in shaping our destiny and our ultimate end. Providentially for us, the Divine will can always find ways to work through all of our choices, even the poorest choices we have willed through our freedom to do so.

The Theology of Providence

Providence occurs, therefore, at the intersection of God's sovereignty or omniscience and our individual human freedom. You cannot emphasize the omniscience of God so strongly that it negates our individual human free will. Neither can you emphasize our free will so much that God is limited and not omniscient and infinite. Therefore you cannot take the design of our own end or the end of history out of God's hands or out of our hands as human beings.

In the designing of our end, God uses all things whether we see them as good or bad, including all of our individual choices. All luck, fortune, or fate may be seen to play a role in our human affairs for good or for bad, but only to the extent that Divine Providence allows in each person's life in the context of history. In fact, it is often that Divine Providence can work better through our mistakes and poor choices than through our wisest and most profound thoughts or good choices.

In his *Theology of Providence*, Rev. Reginald Garrigou-LaGrange O.P. had this to say regarding how Divine Providence directs all things toward their own end and how we should simply abandon ourselves to it like a child holding The Father's hand:

> "Nothing comes to pass but God has foreseen it, willed it or at least permitted it. He wills nothing, permits nothing, unless for the manifestation of His goodness and infinite perfections, for the glory of His Son, and the welfare of those that love Him. In view of these three principles, it is evident that our trust in Providence cannot be too childlike, too steadfast. Indeed, we may go further and say that this trust in Providence should be blind as is our faith, the object of which is those mysteries that are non-evident and unseen (*fides est de non visis*), for we are certain beforehand that Providence is directing all things infallibly to a good purpose, and we are more convinced of the rectitude of His designs than we are of the best of our own intentions" (Garrigan-LaGrange, Part IV).

In Christian thought, all luck, fortune, fate, and coincidence is controlled by Divine Providence. All of these can be pictured as inner circles within the outermost circle, which is Providence. Events that appear to be coincidence, as unconnected or disconnected to us, are known fully to God. This implies that no occurrence in the entire universe is outside of the Divine will of God. God either ordains it or permits it. God does not roll the dice with the universe or any human life and destiny within the universe. Knowledge and foreknowledge, though different to us, are one and the same to the Father. As has been stated previously, in God there is no past or future as God is eternally present.

Only twice in the Gospels do we hear the voice of God, the Father. Once, at the baptism of Jesus and the other time at the Transfiguration of Jesus. Each time, the Father affirms his love for his beloved Son. All of Jesus works and ministry begin with the voice of the Father and the affirmation of His love for him. As adopted sisters and brothers of Jesus and children of the Father, it is entirely possible that at the Second Coming of Jesus we will hear once again the voice of the Father sending forth the Universal Christ with his affirming love at the end of time.

It cannot be fathomed how God can use everything in our lives to bring about the design of our end and our ultimate destiny, mainly because our minds are too finite to fully understand God's providential divine plan. We can only abandon ourselves to it like a child being led by The Father's hand. In Luke 11:1–4, Jesus gives us *The Lord's Prayer* which is considered to be the perfect prayer. Here he asks us to pray to The Father with reverence, respect, and the certainty of a parent's loving and affirming embrace. The prayer can open our hearts as we abandon ourselves to the Divine Providence of God, "Our Father."

There is a supreme intelligence and a divine love, wisdom, and purpose behind Divine Providence which our tiny minds cannot grasp. In the ordering of all things in the universe to their ends, including our own destiny, the mind of God is infinite. Although our minds cannot grasp this providential plan, we can certainly sense it in our spirit. It cannot be "taught;" it can only be "caught."

> "Accept the place the Divine Providence has found for you, the society of your contemporaries, the connection of events." (Ralph Waldo Emerson, *Essays: First Series*)

Chapter Ten

The Coming of the Kingdom of God

Acting in a similar way to what playwrights call "meta-drama," the Kingdom of God is the play within the play of life.

THE REIGN OF GOD

> "Jesus was praying in a certain place, and when he had finished, one of his disciples said to him, 'Lord, teach us to pray just as John taught his disciples.' He said to them, 'When you pray, say: Father, hallowed be your name, your kingdom come . . ." (Luke 11:1–4).

The phrase, "Kingdom of God," appears in the New Testament over one hundred times. The Jewish gospel writer, Matthew, consistently refers to it as "The Kingdom of Heaven." Matthew uses the word "heaven," as a reverential synonym for God and to suggest to the readers of his gospel the end times significance of this divine reality. At the same time, he is primarily emphasizing the partial realization of the Kingdom's earthly reality. Jesus Christ came proclaiming the Kingdom of God, but after his death and resurrection, Jesus became the one proclaimed.

"Kingdom," signifies a state in which God is recognized as the King who reigns and to whom everyone and everything is in submission. The use of the term in the Greek and Hebrew ancient languages denoted the dignity and power of the king. Therefore it is entirely possible that "Kingship" would have been an even better translation. The Kingdom of God was the core of Jesus proclamation, and it was the core of his ministry and mission. Jesus' association of his own person and ministry with the "coming of the kingdom" indicates that he perceives that the Father's great intervention in history has arrived, and that he is the agent of that intervention. Furthermore, it would appear that Jesus repeated use of the self-designated title, "Son of Man," would indicate to his hearers that he has a unique, apocalyptic, and unprecedented role to play in the coming of this Kingdom on earth. His use of the term, because of its historical significance and its rootedness in the Old Testament Book of Daniel, further indicates that there is a future phase to the Kingdom of God which is still to come at the end of history:

> "As the visions during the night continued, I saw one like a Son of Man coming on the clouds of heaven. When he reached the Ancient One and was presented before him, He received dominion, glory, and kingship; nations and peoples of every language serve him. His dominion is an everlasting dominion that shall not be taken away, his kingship shall not be destroyed" (Dan. 7:13–14).

So, "the Kingdom" is not a thing, neither is it a place like worldly kingdoms; it is a person. Jesus is revealing that the Father is fully present within him and because of this, God is present to all those around him. He is the earthly and human manifestation of the divine reality of the Kingdom which is to come and will be fully manifest at the end of time and history and is eternal:

> " . . . and of his Kingdom there will be no end" (Luke 1:33).

PARABLES AND THE KINGDOM

If you want to know the way to enter the Magic Kingdom follow the signs in Disneyland. In much the same manner, if you want to know the way to enter the Kingdom of God follow the signs in the Gospels. Jesus most often spoke of the Kingdom in parables. The parable is a simple word-picture which points the way. The fundamental element which is inherent in the parable is the element of metaphor. A metaphor is a figure of speech in which words or phrases literally denoting certain kinds of objects, ideas, or realities are used in place of others to suggest likeness or analogy between them. This was a method he used to reveal the mystery of the Kingdom to his disciples while at the same time, the meaning and intent of the reality of the Kingdom would remain hidden to many others who heard but did not understand. Even though many heard the words, they did not understand the implication of the words. To form the parables, in creating a miniature word-picture drama, Jesus used things which were from the daily life and world of the people to whom he was speaking. These included several commonplace items such as seeds, weeds, wheat, yeast, treasure, pearls, nets, fish etc. For example:

> "When a large crowd gathered, with people from one town after another journeying to him, he spoke in a parable. 'A sower went out to sow his seed. And

as he sowed, some seed fell on the path and was trampled, and the birds of the sky ate it up. Some seed fell on rocky ground, and when it grew, it withered for lack of moisture. Some seed fell among thorns, and the thorns grew with it and choked it. And some seed fell on good soil, and when it grew, it produced fruit a hundredfold. After saying this, he called out, 'Whoever has ears to hear ought to hear'" (Luke 8:4–8).

In every parable there would be an evident reality along with a mysterious hiddenness which was indicative of the Kingdom. It probably wasn't really Jesus intention to hide the Kingdom from all the hearers; he knew this was simply the result of his preaching the Gospel of the Kingdom in parables. Jesus would later say after reciting the above parable:

"Knowledge of the mysteries of the Kingdom of God has been granted to you, but to the rest they are made known through parables so that they may look but not see, and hear but not understand . . . This is the meaning of the parable . . ." (Luke 8:10–11).

CHILDREN AND THE KINGDOM

In comparing the hearer's receptive attitude to hearing the message of the Kingdom of God, the gospel writers, Matthew, Mark, Luke, and John, often connected wisdom to children as they tell us how wisdom is "vindicated by her children" (Luke 7:35), and how "God hides things from the wise and clever," but "reveals them to little children" (Luke 10:21). In fact, children are mentioned over 100 times by the four gospel writers. But perhaps the most startling example of the use of children in the gospels is when Jesus draws a little child into the midst of the crowd and says:

"Let the children come to me and do not prevent them; for the Kingdom of God belongs to such as these. Amen, I say to you, whoever does not accept the Kingdom of God like a child will not enter it" (Luke 18:16–17).

Jesus is using a child here not so much to illustrate the innocence of children, because as we all know children can be unruly, disobedient, badly behaved, and at times not so very innocent. Jesus is using the example of a little child here to illustrate first what our attitude before the Father needs to be like. Our attitude needs to be like a little child's attitude. We need to become "small" before God. We must be open, receptive, and have the dependent characteristics that a little child has. It also has to do with not only our attitude before God, but also in acknowledging our relationship to the Father as being like a child.

On the other hand, children cover their ears to keep from hearing an unwelcome message or an unpleasant prohibition from a parent. As adults, we sometimes stop-up the ears of our heart to keep from hearing God's voice. In doing this we not only shut out unwelcome news, but the good news of the Kingdom as well.

It is no coincidence that this particular use of a child in the Gospels is placed right after the section where Jesus interacts with the Scribes and Pharisees, whose attitude in stark contrast to the child, is totally the opposite of open, receptive, and dependent. Their attitude is closed, resistant, and unreceptive. They, in fact, refuse to listen to the message of the Kingdom and certainly don't see it or receive it in the example of a little child, illustrating that the message of the Kingdom is really for the simple, the small, and the humble of heart and not for the proud, self-important, high and mighty, or haughty.

St. Therese of Lisieux (St. Therese of the Child Jesus) is a wonderful model of what our attitude should be like as children of the Kingdom of God. To many she seemed foolishly childish, but in fact she taught us that there is real wisdom in having a truly simple love of God, and being obedient as well as willing to be led by the hand of the Holy Spirit. She understood herself to be "a weak little bird with only a light down" but with "an eagle's eyes and heart."

THE CHURCH AS A SACRAMENT OF THE KINGDOM

A sacrament can be called: "a visible sign of an invisible reality." On earth, people make contact with the risen and glorified Christ and through him with God, in and through the community of the Church, as it exists now in time and space. Vatican II stresses that "Christ is always present in his Church and that the church is a sacrament of salvation" (Vatican Council II, *Lumen Gentium*, Ch. VII). So, the Risen Lord exists in history today in the Spirit-filled members of his body and in their actions. Here on earth, the community of believers which is the Church, is his bodily way of existing as the risen and glorified Lord. In Chapter IV on the Laity from Vatican II's *Dogmatic Constitution on the Church* we are told the following as regards the role of the laity in relation to the church and the seeking of the Kingdom:

> "But the laity, by their very vocation, seek the Kingdom of God by engaging in temporal affairs and by ordering them according to the plan of God. They live in the world, that is, in each and in all of the secular professions and occupations. They live in the ordinary circumstances of family and social life, from which the very web of their existence is woven. They are called there by God that by exercising their proper function and led by the spirit of the Gospel they may work for the sanctification of the world from within as a leaven" (Vatican Council II, *Lumen Gentium*, Ch. IV).

In the Bible, several of Paul's Letters refer to the church as "the body of Christ." This is to say that we, as Christians, exist in community as the sacrament of the risen Christ who has the fullness of the Kingdom of God within him. Although we are also a community of sinners and "imperfect saints" we are still all Christ has as his body on earth. As church and as the community of the people of God, we signify the presence of the risen Christ, of his Kingdom, and of his Spirit of saving love:

> "Now you are Christ's body and individually parts of it" (1 Cor. 12:27).

> "And he put all things beneath his feet and gave him as head of all things to the church, which is his body, the fullness of the one who fills all things in every way" (Eph. 1:23).

> "He is the head of the body, the church" (Col. 1:18).

THE KINGDOM; ALREADY, BUT NOT YET

We now live "between the acts." Jesus' predictions of his return make it clear that God's Kingdom is not fully realized. Thus, there is a tremendous tension between understanding that the Kingdom is present now, yet realizing that at one and the same time, it is also futuristic and points to the end of times. Jesus would declare that it is "in your midst" (Luke 17:21); that it had "come near" (Mark 1:15); was "at hand" (Matt. 4:17) and that the Kingdom had "overtaken you" (Matt. 12:28). The implication is that the Kingdom is "already," but it is "not yet." We now live somewhere in between the First and Second Coming of Christ. Our present life can only be understood in terms of not only its connectedness with the past, but also on the basis of its openness and reaching out to the future, a future which for us is uncertain and unknown. Our essence therefore, is not only that of a "human being," but also that of a "human becoming." In fact, one of the ways we are told that we can enter the Kingdom, for example, is to "become like a little child" (Matt. 18:1–3).

Jesus was the Sacrament of God. Following the earthly ministry of Jesus, the Kingdom will be present in the church through the indwelling Holy Spirit. The church would be the Sacrament of the Kingdom. Although this is certainly true, the Kingdom will not be fully realized in the church until the Second Coming of Christ at the end of time. The Kingdom is then, both the process and the ultimate reality which will occur at the end of time as it unifies reality and mystery. So, the Kingdom of God had its beginning at creation, reached its zenith or climax in Jesus Christ and will be brought to finality and completion at the parousia with the Second Coming of Christ.

KINGDOM POWER; THE ETERNALITY OF LOVE

"God is love" (1 John 4:8).

The above scripture verse tells us much about the very essence of God. If God is love then the Kingdom of God must be a Kingdom of love. We can only understand the divine love which creates, sustains, and now permeates the kingdom by its analogies to human love. How can we possibly comprehend that God loved the world so much as to give his only Son (John 3:16)?

Kingdom love is not only eternal it is unconditional, dynamic, essentially active, life giving, self-sacrificing and universal. It is a true love in every sense of the word.

For the Kingdom of God which is in our midst on earth, it is love which has the power to transform those who live in the Kingdom as a present reality and wait expectantly for the return of Christ and the fullness of the future coming of the Kingdom. The scriptures tell us:

"God is love, and whoever remains in love remains in God and God in them" (1 John 4:16).

As Christians, we can believe that Jesus as the Sacrament of God is the expression of God's perfect love for the world. Love is the essence and existence of God. The scriptures, from beginning to end, enable us to draw this fundamental conclusion about the essence and existence of God. Love is also the self-communication of God and the spiritual dynamic within us as people of God. It is furthermore, the ultimate reality of being; it is eternal and never dies. It will be all there is in the end:

"So faith, hope, love remain, these three; but the greatest of these is love" (1 Cor. 13:13).

If this is true, then we must conclude that the primary characteristic of God's eternal Kingdom is also love. The Kingdom is a realm of love and you cannot open the door to the Kingdom without the key of love. While we speak about God's kingdom coming in power, it is in the power of love that God's kingdom can transform the world. It is God in the Holy Spirit present in our hearts that gives us the power to love. It is in our loving relationships each and every day that God lives and the fullness of the Kingdom is present to us and is being realized. Love is the theme of the play of life.

It is in loving another or loving others that we orient ourselves to God in the spirit and assist in building his Kingdom. Love is not anonymous and we cannot love God without loving other persons. When the Kingdom of God assumes a personal face and heart for us as we love another, that love for the personal "other" has universal implications and consequences for the Kingdom. To quote Karl Rahner:

> "In love all the powers of my soul flow out toward you, wanting never more to return, but to lose themselves completely in you, since by your love you are the inmost center of my heart, closer to me than I am to myself" (*Encounters With Silence*).

LOVE AND THE OMEGA POINT

In his most profound book, *The Phenomenon of Man*, Teilhard de Chardin discusses the attributes of the Omega Point. The first attribute of the Omega he mentions is that of Love. At the Omega Point the cosmos and consciousness are seen to converge upon the Universal Christ as God becomes all in all. Teilhard's basic premise is that all of reality—the whole of the cosmic order—is converging and spiritually evolving, as it flows out and moves toward a final goal. All of history is therefore in movement toward the Universal Christ. The author writes:

> "First of all the 'reason of love.' Expressed in terms of internal energy, the cosmic function of Omega consists in initiating and maintaining within its radius the unanimity of the world's reflective particles. But how could it exercise this action were it not in some sort loving and lovable at this very moment? Love, I said dies in contact with the impersonal and the anonymous . . . With love, as with every other sort of energy, it is within the existing datum that the lines of force must at every instant come together . . . To be supremely attractive, Omega must be extremely present" (de Chardin, *The Phenomenon of Man*, 269).

The reign of God will be fully realized at the end of time and history with the Second Coming of Christ. That implies a situation where everything in the universe . . . every person in the world and the whole of creation . . . would be living under the dynamic rule of God's love. In the eternal Kingdom of God, love will rule all; it will prevail and then permeate everything in the universe as it radiates:

> "Then the seventh angel blew his trumpet. There were loud voices in heaven saying, 'The kingdom of the world now belongs to our Lord and to his anointed, and he will reign forever and ever" (Rev. 11:15).

Chapter Eleven

The Second Coming;
The End Times Role of Jesus Christ

Jesus Christ is the central Hero in the play of life and thus has the lead role.

THE PAROUSIA

Parousia (/pəˈruːziə/; Greek: παρουσία) is pronounced "pair-oo-see-ah" and is an ancient Greek word meaning presence, arrival, or official visit. It refers to the physical arrival of a person or hero. The word also refers to the manifestation of a divine presence. In Christian theology, its meaning refers to the physical presence and arrival of Jesus Christ at the Second Coming. Christians have always believed that Jesus Christ, as Savior, would come back to close the current period of human history on earth and usher in the fullness of the Kingdom of God. The Parousia, the Second Coming of Christ, is the central event in all of Christian eschatology or the study of the "last things."

PAROUSIA, OLD TESTAMENT TO NEW

The Parousia was first prophetically described in terms of Old Testament apocalyptic passages and images, for example, in the books of Isaiah and Daniel. Later, in fact, as the New Testament develops these Old Testament images, Jesus will apply the title "Son of man" as his most characteristic way of referring to himself. The Second Coming of Christ described in the New Testament, particularly in 1 & 2 Thessalonians (1 Thes. 2:19; 3:13; 4:15; 5:23; 2 Thes. 2:1, 8, 9) was seen to replace many of the Old Testament references to what was called, "The Day of Yahweh" (Amos 5:18; Joel 2:1).

"The stars and constellations of the heavens send forth no light; the sun is dark when it rises, and the light of the moon does not shine . . . The heavens shall be rolled up like a scroll" (Isa. 13:10; 34:4).

"As the visions during the night continued, I saw One like the son of man coming on the clouds of heaven; When he reached the Ancient One and was presented before him, He received dominion, glory, and kingship; nations and peoples of every language serve him. His dominion is an everlasting dominion that shall not be taken away, his kingship shall not be destroyed" (Dan. 7:13–14).

PAROUSIA, NEW TESTAMENT

In the New Testament the Second Coming of Christ as Judge of the world, is an oft-repeated doctrine. The gospels foretell this event and graphically portray its circumstances:

"For just as lightening comes from the east and is seen as far away as the west, so will the coming of the Son of Man be." And "When the Son of Man comes in his glory and all the angels with him, he will sit upon his glorious throne, and all the nations will be assembled before him" (Matt. 24:27; 25:31).

The Apostles, including St. Paul, also give a most prominent place to this doctrine in their preaching and writings in the New Testament. For example (Acts 10:42; 17:31; Rom. 2:5–16; 14:10; 1 Cor. 4:5; 2 Cor. 5:10; 2 Tim. 4:1; 2 Thes. 1:5; Jas. 5:7).

Besides the name Parousia, or Advent (1 Cor. 15:23; 2 Thes. 2:19), the Second Coming is also called Epiphany, Epiphaneia, or Appearance. For example (2 Thes. 2:8; 1 Tim. 6:14; 2 Tim. 4:1; Tit. 2:13). Several references to the Second Coming of Christ also appear in the Book of Revelation which is focused primarily on the Second Coming and the reign of the Universal Christ.

The time of the Second Coming is also spoken of as "that Day" (2 Tim. 4:8), "the day of the Lord" (1 Thes. 5:2), "the day of Christ" (Phil. 1:6; 2:16), "the day of the Son of Man" (Luke 17:30), and "the last day" (John 6:39–40).

MORAL DEPRAVITY AND SOCIAL WICKEDNESS

"Religious and moral truths fall more in the province of conscience than that of intellect" (Newman 149).

The New Testament also reveals that prior to this, there will exist a condition of moral depravity, doctrinal error, and false teaching which will be devoid of the true spirit of religion that will prevail in the final days leading up to the Second Coming. When moral law is violated, it contributes to the increase of moral depravity. Moral law only requires love . . . of the true self and love of both God and fellow man. It involves free choices which take place in the will and love's power to choose the good. Its ultimate choosing is of the highest well-being of God, humankind, and of the universe.

Christ did predict that social wickedness would increase prior to his return. Many conditions we currently see all around us show the signs of increasing moral depravity. For example, the widespread outbreak of urban violence exploding in countries around the world indicates that crime is increasingly running rampant. It seems that every few weeks a mass murder occurs someplace. Our city streets are no longer safe. We have over 2,000,000 inmates incarcerated in the United States alone. Our prisons are now so full of hardened inmates, that we don't have the adequate facilities to even house them any longer and must often turn them out to prey on innocent people once again.

Because we have rejected religious truth and the foundation of all that is good, we no longer even know the difference between good and evil, virtue or vice. One of the most disturbing signs of moral depravity that exists today is in the modern effort to subordinate the church to the state. For example, the government is currently pressing religious employers and individuals to violate their core moral and religious beliefs as well as their consciences concerning human life. The intervention of the state in the internal life of many religious institutions is not only a sign of the times in regards to increasing moral depravity, but is also weakening personal freedoms and the freedom of the church. Without freedom there can be no love and love is the basis of not only all that is moral, but all that is good.

Doctrinal error and false teaching also abound and is tickling people's ears in many of our churches. Our consciences have become so scarred, we are no longer offended by wickedness but tolerate it. Since virtually all such perverted behavior people engage in is now categorized under "normal behavior," the door is now open for even much stranger and perverted behavior to become the accepted norm.

Years ago we would have been outraged by the decadence and debauchery that daily fills our streets, shows on television, movie screens, music and art, video games, business practices, and political chambers. So much fills the news media that is appalling to many of us that we don't even want to read about it or watch it on television any longer. In fact, we have gotten so used to such increases in moral depravity that most of us no longer even speak out against it.

As a society, we have increasingly accepted such things as illicit sexual relationships, promiscuity, abortion, discourtesy, unkindness, impoliteness, crookedness, lying, stealing, philandering, easy divorce, euthanasia, and even in some circumstances, torture or murder. We have gotten so used to political corruption and financial mismanagement that we continue to re-elect corrupt officials back into office over and over again. Business people who steal mercilessly from everyone, including widows, orphans, and the elderly, thumb their noses and seem often to get off repeatedly with just a slap on the hand. What Gordon Gekko said, "Greed is good," has become a watchword in business.

Giving one's word or handshake agreements have now become meaningless to many. Things like honor, chastity, integrity, and virtue have become subjects of ridicule, scorn, and are often considered even laughable. The Golden Rule, "Do unto others as you would have them do unto you."(Luke 6:31) has been replaced with the shortened version of just simply, "Do unto others."

The visible role models many of us have today in the sports world, entertainment industry, politics, and business and industry are often among the most morally depraved people. They are our modern icons.

"What's in it for me?" has become the national outcry for increasing numbers of people in society. Yet the scriptures warn us that:

> "Because of the increase of evil doing, the love of many will grow cold" (Matt. 24:12,).

Morality denotes those concrete activities which may be defined as human conduct in so far as it is freely subordinated to the ideals of what is right and loving. But the love of many is, in fact, growing cold. This necessitates a call for love which will cover "a multitude of sins" as love is permanent. Even when faith yields to seeing and hope yields to realizing, love will be all there is for any of us at the end of times before Christ comes. Love and prayer as well as our life's example is all any of us really have to combat the moral decline evident in society. Scripture warns us:

> "But understand this: there will be terrifying times in the last days. People will be self-centered and lovers of money, proud, haughty, abusive, disobedient to their parents, ungrateful, irreligious, callous, implacable, slanderous, licentious, brutal, hating what is good, traitors, reckless, conceited, lovers of pleasure rather than lovers of God, as they make a pretense of religion but deny its power. Reject them" (2 Tim. 3:1–5).

> "The end of all things is at hand. Therefore be serious and sober for prayers. Above all, let your love for one another be intense, because love covers a multitude of sins" (1 Pet. 4:7–8).

> "So faith, hope, love remain, these three; but the greatest of these is love" (1 Cor. 13:13).

COSMIC TURBULENCE

There is also a cosmic aspect to the Parousia. There will be birth pangs and convulsions in nature and in history prior to the messianic era and the ushering in of the Second Coming of Christ . . . widespread wars, earthquakes and famines, signs in the sun, moon, and stars as well as the natural realm on earth. The seas will roar. There will be, in effect, an upheavel of the cosmos. The scriptures exhort us to vigilance.

> "But in those days after that tribulation the sun will be darkened, and the moon will not give its light, and the stars will be falling from the sky, and the powers in the heavens will be shaken. And then they will see 'the Son of Man' coming in the clouds with great power and glory . . ." (Mark 13:24–26).

Wars, famines, and earthquakes have been occurring throughout the history of life on this planet. What seems to be described here is a tremendous increase in the frequency and intensity of these events. As far as the sun being darkened, we do know that we need the sun's light. We also need its heat and its energy which gives rise to all life on earth. Without the sun, life on earth would eventually die out soon after the sun's dying out. Of course without being able to reflect the sun's light, the moon would turn dark as well. The moon controls the movement of the seas and the tides; the seas would certainly roar. As far as stars falling from the sky . . . who knows what disturbances would occur in synchronization with all these other tremendous disruptions in the universe as "the heavens are shaken."

PREPARATIONS FOR THE PAROUSIA

It was the Apostle Paul who was the originator of the Christian term, "Parousia," in the New Testament, to describe Christ's Second Coming. Paul, most particularly, continually exhorted Christians to readiness through vigilance and the leading of a virtuous life in preparation for the Parousia. To Paul, the Christian life should be lived in the hope and expectancy of the Second Coming. For him, the most important aspect of the Parousia is the fulfillment of union with Christ. Seventeen verses in the New Testament refer to the Second Coming of Christ, except the one case in which it refers to the coming of the "Day of God" (2 Pet. 3:11–13). Paul tells us to be prepared:

> "Since everything is to be dissolved in this way, what sort of persons ought you to be, conducting yourselves in holiness and devotion, waiting for and hastening the coming of the day of God, because of which the heavens will be dissolved in flames and the elements melted by fire. According to his promise

we await new heavens and a new earth in which righteousness dwells" (2 Pet. 3:11–13).

"As he was sitting on the Mount of Olives, the disciples approached him privately and said, 'Tell us when will this happen, and what sign will there be of your coming and of the end of the age? Jesus said to them in reply, 'See that no one deceives you. For many will come in my name, saying 'I am the Messiah,' and they will deceive many. You will hear of wars and reports of wars; see that you are not alarmed, for these things must happen, but it will not yet be the end. Nation will rise against nation, and kingdom against kingdom; there will be famines and earthquakes from place to place. All these are the beginning of the labor pains . . . For just as lightening comes from the east and is seen as far away as the west, so will the coming of the Son of Man be. Wherever the corpse is there the vultures will gather. Immediately after the tribulation of those days, the sun will be darkened, and the moon will not give its light, and the stars will fall from the sky, and the powers of the heavens will be shaken. And then the sign of the Son of Man will appear in the heaven, and all the tribes of the earth will mourn, and they will see The Son of Man coming upon the clouds of heaven with power and great glory'" (Matt. 24:3–8, 27–30).

"For just as in Adam all die, so too in Christ shall all be brought to life, but each one in proper order: Christ the first fruits; then at his coming, those who belong to Christ; then comes the end, when he hands over the kingdom to his God and Father when he has destroyed every sovereignty and every authority and power" (1 Cor. 15:22–24).

"For what is our hope or joy or crown to boast of in the presence of our Lord Jesus at his coming if not you yourselves? For you are our glory and joy . . . So as to strengthen your hearts, to be blameless in holiness before our God and Father at the coming of our Lord Jesus with all his holy ones . . . Indeed, we tell you this, on the word of the Lord, that we who are alive, who are left until the coming of the Lord, will surely not precede those who have fallen asleep. For the Lord himself with the word of command, with the voice of an archangel and with the trumpet of God, will come down from heaven, and the dead in Christ will rise first. Then we who are alive, who are left, will be caught up together with them in the clouds to meet the Lord in the air. Thus we shall always be with the Lord . . . May the God of peace himself make you perfectly holy and may you entirely, spirit, soul, and body, be preserved blameless for the coming of our Lord Jesus Christ" (1 Thes. 2:19; 3:13; 4:15–17; 5:23).

"We ask you, brothers and sisters, with regard to the coming of our Lord Jesus Christ and our assembling with him, not to be shaken out of your minds suddenly, or to be alarmed either by a 'spirit,' or by an oral statement or by a letter allegedly from us to the effect that the day of the Lord is at hand . . . And then the lawless one will be revealed, who the Lord Jesus will kill with the breath of his mouth and render powerless by the manifestation of his coming . . ." (2 Thes. 2:1, 8).

"Be patient, therefore, brothers and sisters, until the coming of the Lord" (Jas. 5:7).

"We did not follow cleverly devised myths when we made known to you the power and coming of our Lord Jesus Christ, but we had been eyewitnesses of his majesty . . . Know this first of all, that in the last days scoffers will come to scoff, living according to their own desires and saying, 'Where is the promise of his coming? . . . Since everything is to be dissolved in this way, what sort of persons ought you to be, conducting yourselves in holiness and devotion, waiting for and hastening the coming of the Day of God because of which the heavens will be dissolved in flames and the elements melted by fire. But according to his promise we await new heavens and a new earth in which righteousness dwells'" (2 Pet. 1:16; 3:4, 11–13).

"And now, children, remain in him, so that when he appears we may have confidence and not be put to shame by him at his coming" (1 John 2:28).

PAROUSIA: WHEN?

The Parousia created a crisis in the early Christian community who regarded it as imminent. After the death of Jesus of Nazareth, many believed that the Second Coming of Christ would occur in their lifetimes. There are many scoffers today as well who ridicule the promise of the Parousia particularly because of the apparent delay. But no one knows exactly when the Second Coming of Jesus Christ will occur as this is known only to the Father. We should avoid pointless speculations about the time, the details of the signs, the nature of the difficulties, etc. As Christians we should live our lives in the hope and expectation of Christ's coming. We should focus instead on the need for living the Gospel so as to be prepared for the Parousia whenever it happens and ultimately be prepared to come before the judgment seat of God.

The visible coming of Christ in power and glory will be the signal for the rising of the dead. All the dead who are to be judged will rise, the wicked as well as the just. According to the scriptures, there is to be only one simultaneous general resurrection, for the good and the bad. Regarding the qualities of the risen bodies, in the case of the just we have St. Paul's description in 1 Corinthians 15 (cf. Matt. 13:43; Phil. 3:21), but in the case of the damned we can only affirm that their bodies will be incorruptible. We are all to be judged by a loving, just, and merciful God.

Finally, the Book of Revelation, the final book of the Bible, ends with a simple prayer. In Aramaic, the words are, "Marana tha," which means, "Our Lord, come" (Rev. 22:20). When the Lord Jesus Christ does come, the Parousia will merge history with eschatology as history ends and we enter fully into the glory which awaits in eternity with our Lord and Savior, Jesus Christ. The salvific role of the Universal Christ and judgment will be the central themes of the Parousia. The Second Coming of Christ will be the grand opening scene as the curtain rises for the final act of the play of life.

Chapter Twelve

Justice and Mercy at the Judgment Seat of Christ

THE JUDGMENT SEAT

"For we must all appear before the judgment seat of Christ, so that each one may receive recompense, according to what he did in the body, whether good or evil" (2 Cor. 5:10).

In other of the Apostle Paul's Letters, (ex. Rom. 14:10), he refers to this as 'the judgment seat of God.' Paul freely interspersed Christ and God in referring to the judgment seat, as he believed Christ is God.

At the end of time and history, following the Second Coming of Christ, we will come before the judgment seat of God in Christ. The purpose of the judgment seat of Christ is an evaluation of how we had lived our total lives. It is a particular judgment. The things we did in the dark and in secret will be brought out into the light of day as the light of Christ shines on us. Our inner beings will be open and revealed before God. As the above scripture verse states: "each may receive recompense, according to what he did in the body, whether good or evil."

WHAT IS JUSTICE?

Much of the material in the *Summa* of St. Thomas Aquinas is drawn from the works of the ancient philosopher Aristotle. And justice is the only virtue to which Aristotle devoted an entire book (Aristotle, *Nicomachean Ethics*, Book V). He considered it one of the Cardinal Virtues. Often referencing Aristotle, Thomas Aquinas has said in his *Summa*:

"The world was not made in justice" (Aquinas, I, Q 21, 4).

St Thomas saw the justice of God to be an accompaniment to God's good-ness and a dimension of God's essence. In God's creation of the world, which was created from nothing, God did not "owe" anything to anyone as a matter of justice. In particular, God did not owe anyone their very existence. But if created existence is not due to a matter of justice, it must be due to something higher than or beyond justice. Our existence is more comparable to a loving gift than like something we should consider as a right under justice. So, the conclusion St Thomas seems to make is that the world was created in love and mercy, not justice, but certainly not without justice.

Justice secured a God-given time for each of us to receive reward or punishment at the end of time and history at the judgment seat of God. In the scriptures, "justice" and "righteousness" are closely connected. Justice is seen to render to each and all what belongs rightly to them. In fact, in the Old Testament, they are both translated from the same Hebrew word, *sedeqa,* and God's justice and righteousness is revealed to us through creation and through the Law and the Prophets. In turn, for us to be considered just and righteous before God, we would need to fulfill our duties and responsibilities to God, others, and our true selves. Justice is seen to be an interior relation-ship to God which is fulfilled through exterior duties and responsibilities in personal relationships and in society.

In the New Testament, in the light of Christ, justice is seen to flow from love. Jesus Christ, through his death on the cross and his rising, is found to be the embodiment and personification of both God's Divine Justice and Divine Love. He is also seen as the fulfillment of the Law and the Prophets as well. The fact that Christ underwent the passion of the crucifixion represents both a superabundance of both justice and love—justice, because the sins of man-kind are compensated for, and love because Jesus endured this terrible suffer-ing and death for our sake to show his love for us. Therefore, the Christian understanding of justice cannot be viewed merely as the performance of a series of rights, duties, and responsibilities. It cannot be understood apart from the Holy Spirit sent by God, the Father and Jesus, and now abiding within the people of God, giving God's grace and power for any of us to be just and loving before God. So, justice is based on love, flows from it, and in its return tends toward it.

The late Fr. Theodore Hesburgh, the former President of Notre Dame University, had a favorite prayer which he recited as grace before many of his meals. It is as follows:

"O God, to those who have hunger, give bread. And to us who have bread, give the hunger for justice."

WHAT IS MERCY?

Of all the plays Shakespeare ever wrote, my favorite has always been *The Merchant of Venice* and one particular line of the play has always resonated with me:

> "The quality of mercy is not strained, dropping as the gentle rain from heaven" (Shakespeare, *Merchant of Venice*, Act IV: Sc I).

There is tremendous conflict in this play between justice and mercy. It is a key theme of the play itself as Shakespeare emphasizes how mercy blesses both the giver and the receiver and is most powerful when it is granted by one who holds the power over another. To the giver, mercy is more important than the power itself. And finally, toward the end of the play, Shakespeare makes the point that earthly power most resembles God's power when justice is guided by mercy.

If the world were only a just world, it would unfortunately be a giftless world. A gift is the giving or receiving of something that is not owed. Mercy is a gift of a giving God. Ultimately, God "for-gives." It is said that, as human beings and children of God, it is virtually impossible for us to outgive God. If we wish to imitate the mercy of God, all we can do is forgive (for-give). Mercy depends on God's extension of unmerited grace to us. It can never be earned as it is never owed.

The word, *mercy,* came into our language from the Latin word, *merced*, which means "the price paid for something." Therefore, God's mercy implies that God has paid the price for us to receive the gift. In our case, it also implies that Jesus Christ, God's Son, through his dying and rising was the price paid for our sins to be for-given. Jesus Christ, as God's Divine Mercy, is God's gift to the world.

Mercy, as a gift of God, shows not only God's love for us, but also his kindness and compassion. With God, mercy is much wider than merely forgiveness from an all-powerful God. It also shows God's kind and compassionate forbearance toward us as offenders.

Mercy is also illustrative of God's patience with us as offenders, as endurance is a form of patience and we are told over 30 times in the Psalms alone:

> "God's mercy endures forever." (Ps. 106, 107, 118, 136, 138).

Thomas Aquinas maintained the following as regards the theology behind the reconciliation of the mercy and justice of God:

> "God acts mercifully, not indeed by going against His justice, but by doing something more than justice; thus a man who pays another two hundred pieces of money, though owing him only one hundred, does nothing against justice,

but acts liberally or mercifully. The case is the same with one who pardons an offence committed against him, for in remitting it he may be said to bestow a gift. Hence the Apostle calls remission a forgiving: 'Forgive one another, as Christ has forgiven you (Eph. 4:32).' Hence it is clear that mercy does not destroy justice, but in a sense is the fullness thereof. And thus it is said: 'Mercy exalts itself above judgment'" (Jas. 2:13) (Aquinas, I, Q 21, 3).

On October 25, 2015, Pope Francis closed this past year's Synod on the Family by calling for a "more merciful, less judgmental church." He also said to all those in attendance, including the 275 Synod fathers, "Today is a time of mercy." Ultimately, he declared that beginning with the church year on December 8, 2015, that this would be a Jubilee Year of Mercy in the Catholic church.

RECONCILING JUSTICE AND MERCY AT THE END OF TIME

Infinitely just and infinitely merciful describes a character trait of a loving God. Without the reconciling of justice and mercy, God could not be God. When justice is retributive, mercy is rehabilitative. When justice demands punishment, mercy forbears. Following the death and resurrection of Jesus Christ, justice and mercy will always be reconciled, as well as interdependent and interactive. This implies that God cannot be just without being merciful, nor can God be merciful without being just. As we each and all come before the judgment seat of God, we should be expecting both, as we will receive both, but it is only mercy that will be God's gift.

On the other hand, justice also demands that the other be given what they deserve by right. That is why feeding the hungry, sheltering the homeless, visiting the sick or imprisoned, and forgiving offenses are seen as "works of mercy," while at the same time they render justice by right.

But God's mercy goes even beyond merely what people deserve by right; it gives as a gift of God, more than we justly deserve, in that we are forgiven. God's mercy seasons God's justice and makes it perfect in love. The just God shows his love for us through his mercy and forgiveness. Human justice is pictured in art as a blindfolded woman carrying scales and a sword. This indicates that, in the law, justice must be emotionally impassive and completely unmoved by the pathos of the actual situation. However, under the law, human mercy gives one the power to feel.

It is similar with God's justice and God's mercy. If justice is the fulfillment of the law and renders reward or punishment unemotionally, impassively, and without regard to the person in the situation, God's mercy can only be seen as more than the fulfillment of the law in that it is the spirit of the law. God's mercy and God's justice are then reconciled through the Spirit of God, the Holy Spirit. Then God's mercy becomes God's justice and God's justice is God's mercy. As children of God, who will each and every one of us, be judged by God in the end at the judgment seat of God, we will receive both God's justice and God's mercy in full measure.

While growing up in East Boston, I often recall a statement my dad used to make about his future dying. He used to say: "When I die and come face to face before God, I would never ask God for justice, only mercy." He said that he believed that if he asked for God's justice that God would grant it to him by right, but then he was convinced that he wouldn't be happy with what he got. Those were wise words and I will never forget them. My dad has since passed on, and I'm assuming that at his turn before God at the judgment seat, he asked for only God's mercy and received what he asked for from a just and merciful God who loves him. I hope to do the same when I come before God for judgment.

Finally, justice and mercy are united in Christ, for it is only through the recognition of our own sinfulness that God can offer us God's mercy. However, If we do not see ourselves as sinners, then what need do we have for mercy? Lord, please have mercy on me, a sinner.

Chapter Thirteen

The Resurrection of the Body

"As they were coming down from the mountain, he charged them not to relate what they had seen to anyone, except when the Son of Man had risen from the dead. So they kept the matter to themselves, questioning what rising from the dead meant" (Mark 9:9–10).

Anyone who writes about resurrection of the body cannot know with full certainty all that the subject matter entails. How can the caterpillar describe fully, the experience of what the butterfly's body will be like? So, I write as one who has formed his thinking based only on a set of beliefs in bodily resurrection conveyed to me from a thorough reading of scripture and handed on to me through theological investigation, the direction of the Holy Spirit, and Church Tradition. Creation has evidenced that God is the Source, Prime Mover, and Alpha of all reality. But it will be our own bodily resurrection that will evidence for us that God, in Christ is the unifying end point and Omega of all reality.

BODILINESS

What the experience of bodily resurrection will actually be like in the end will be the best teacher. But the body is intrinsic to the "beingness" of the human person. We are not just embodied spirits, we are whole persons and our bodiliness implies more than flesh alone. In fact, the scriptures use two different Greek words; *sarx* for flesh and *soma* for body. As whole persons, we are either oriented toward God or away from God. It is the sins of our flesh which orients us away from God.

At the end of our time on this earth, the flesh, because of our sins, will be put to death:

"For the concern of the flesh is hostility toward God; it does not submit to the law of God, nor can it; and those who are in the flesh cannot please God. But you are not in the flesh; on the contrary, you are in the spirit, if only the Spirit of God dwells in you. Whoever does not have the Spirit of Christ does not belong to him. But if Christ is in you, although the body is dead because of sin, the spirit is alive because of righteousness. If the Spirit of the one who raised Jesus from the dead dwells in you, the one who raised Christ from the dead will give life to your mortal bodies also, through his Spirit that dwells in you" (Rom. 8:7–11).

The old self is governed by the flesh and the flesh will die, but the new self is governed by the Spirit and will experience a resurrection of the body on the last day through having lived a life in the Spirit. To be fully human and fully alive is to be living "in the Spirit" now, while awaiting our new and glorified body on the last day as we are raised up.

OLD TESTAMENT AND RESURRECTION

Without spending too much time on other religions for now, let us simply say that the Judeo-Christian religion was not the first to believe in bodily resurrection. Many of the other ancient religions did as well. If scripture must be our primary starting point for now, then we first find evidence of a developing belief that the dead will rise in a bodily resurrection in the Old Testament Prophetic books and the Wisdom literature:

> "And many of those who sleep in the dust of the earth shall awake; some shall live forever, and some shall be an everlasting horror and disgrace" (Dan. 12:2).

> "And you shall know that I am the Lord, when I open your graves, and have you rise from them, O my people" (Ezek. 37:13).

> " . . . But your dead shall live, their corpses shall rise; awake and sing, you who lie in the dust" (Isa. 26:19).

> "But as for me, I know that my Vindicator lives, and that he will at last stand forth upon the dust; Whom I myself shall see: my own eyes, not another's shall behold him and from my flesh I shall see God; my inmost being is consumed with longing" (Job 19:25–27).

So, resurrection was seen even then as the rising again from the dead, the resumption of life. But in the Old Testament, these are prophetic words and no one actually 'rose from the dead' and spoke to others about the experience until the time of Jesus of Nazareth.

NEW TESTAMENT AND RESURRECTION

In many ways, the mystery of Jesus resurrection enlightened the Apostles and the early Christian church. It allowed them to see Christ's life and death from a totally different perspective and in a whole new way. The resurrection of Jesus was essentially, an evolution of consciousness for the disciples of the early church.

The fact that Jesus' resurrection was not just something spiritual but also a bodily resurrection is clear from the fact that several of the gospels tell us that after the resurrection, Jesus touched (John 20:27), ate (Luke 24:41–43), and spoke (John 21:15–22) with the disciples and also that Thomas put his fingers in his nail marked hands and in his side (John 20:27). This allowed the early church to combat several of the Gnostic heresies which were circulating, attempting to make of Jesus' resurrection something purely spiritual and not a bodily resurrection. It is also evident that there was clearly something very different about the "bodiliness" of Jesus following the resurrection as the disciples couldn't recognize him at first. It is indicated that Jesus coming and going was also very different. Furthermore, we are told specifically in Mark's gospel that Jesus appeared in another form:

> "After this he appeared in another form to two of them walking along on their way to the country" (Mark 16:12).

So, even though it was seen to be Jesus resurrected body, his glorified body was different from his body prior to the crucifixion. Paul confirms that we also will have a different "bodiliness" after the resurrection of the dead, but that we will have a body none the less and it will be our new body:

> "But some will say, 'How are the dead raised? With what kind of body will they come back?' You fool! What you sow is not brought to life unless it dies. And what you sow is not the body that is to be but a bare kernel of wheat, perhaps or some other kind; but God gives it a body as he chooses, and to each of the seeds its own body . . . So also is the resurrection of the dead. It is sown corruptible; it is raised incorruptible. It is sown dishonorable; it is raised glorious. It is sown weak; it is raised powerful. It is sown a natural body; it is raised a spiritual body. If there is a natural body, there is also a spiritual one" (1 Cor. 15:35–38; 42–44).

The New Testament proclaims that the visible coming (parousia) of Christ in power and glory will be the signal for the rising of the dead. The resurrection of the dead was expressly taught by Christ in the gospels:

> "Do not be amazed at this, because an hour is coming in which all who are in the tombs will hear his voice." And

"For this is the will of my Father, that everyone who sees the Son and believes in him may have eternal life, and I shall raise him on the last day."

"Jesus told her 'I am the resurrection and the life; whoever believes in me, even if he dies, will live, and everyone who lives and believes in me will never die. Do you believe this?" (John 5:28–29; 6:40; 11:25–26)

St. Paul as well, places the general resurrection of the dead on the same level of certainty with that of Christ's Resurrection. All the dead who are to be judged will rise, the wicked as well as the just. Regarding the qualities of the risen bodies in the case of the just we have St. Paul's description in Romans 8, 1 Corinthians 15, and Phillipians 3 as a basis, but in the case of the damned we can only affirm that their bodies will rise as well, yet not be necessarily glorious:

"He will change our lowly body to conform with his glorified body by the power that enables him also to bring all things into subjection to himself" (Phil. 3:21).

"If the Spirit of the one who raised Jesus from the dead dwells in you, the one who raised Christ from the dead will give life to your mortal bodies also, through his Spirit that dwells in you" (Rom. 8:11).

"If Christ be preached, that he rose again from the dead, how do some among you say that there is no resurrection of the dead? But if there be no resurrection of the dead, then Christ is not risen again. And if Christ be not risen again, then is our preaching vain, and your faith is also vain" (1 Cor. 15:12).

EARLY CHRISTIAN CHURCH AND RESURRECTION

Since the first centuries of the early Christian church we have proclaimed this belief that the dead will rise in both the Nicene Creed and the Athanasian Creed:

"We confess one baptism for the forgiveness of sins; we look for a resurrection of the dead and life in the age to come. Amen" (Nicene Creed).

"Jesus Christ sits at the right hand of God the Father Almighty. From there he shall come to judge the living and the dead; at his coming all men have to rise again with their bodies and will render an account of their own deeds; and those who have done good will go into life everlasting, but those who have done evil, into eternal fire" (Athanasian Creed).

The risen body of all, the just and the wicked, will have its own identity. We will all rise whole and entire to immortality. But the risen bodies of the just will be distinguished not only by their incorruption, but also their glorification, brilliance, agility in movement, and spirituality. We are told this as well by St. Paul in chapter 15 of 1st Corinthians. As the body is the partner of the soul's crimes and the close companion of her virtues, the justice of God would seem to demand that the body be the sharer in the soul's punishment or reward. Furthermore, although it is indicated that our bodies will be changed and transformed as Jesus body was, it would destroy the very idea of resurrection if the dead were to rise in bodies not their own.

For the most part, the New Testament speaks to the resurrection of the dead and not necessarily to a resurrection of the flesh. Paul makes clear that he did not believe that the flesh could rise:

> "This I declare, brothers and sisters: flesh and blood cannot inherit the Kingdom of God, nor does corruption inherit incorruption" (1 Cor. 15:50).

As persons, we are more than flesh and blood and certainly more than embodied spirits. In resurrection of the body, our hope is that our whole being will be resurrected as we are given a new body. However, there was some confusion created with the distinction between flesh and body in the writings of many of the early church Fathers. These included Clement, Irenaeus, Justin Martyr, and Augustine. They gave continuous evidence that what we should expect is a whole body resurrection:

> "Indeed, God calls even the body to resurrection and promises it everlasting life. When he promises to save the man, he thereby makes his promise to the flesh. What is man but a rational living being composed of soul and body? Is the soul by itself a man? No, it is but the soul of a man. Can the body be called a man? No, it can but be called the body of a man. If, then, neither of these is by itself a man, but that which is composed of the two together is called a man, and if God has called man to life and resurrection, he has called not a part, but the whole, which is the soul and the body" (Lebreton "Justin Martyr").

THE ASSUMPTION

The dogma of the Assumption pertaining to Mary, the Mother of God, tells us much about the resurrection of the body. The Assumption should not be viewed as a personal privilege given to Mary in light of her role as Mother of God or due to her because of her purity and holiness from the time of her Immaculate Conception. It should be viewed in light of Mary's wider role on earth and in heaven as well as the mission of her life. Mary is an icon of the church. Her call to union in heaven with God in Christ in the totality of her human existence, body and soul, asserts something about human existence being in part, bodily existence as well as spiritual existence. The resurrection of the body, based on the Assumption of Mary tells us there is a promise of both bodily and material existence as well as a spiritual existence that awaits us.

CATHOLIC CATECHISM AND RISING

The Catechism of the Catholic Church has reiterated the teaching of the resurrection of the body at the end of time on the last day, stating the what, who, how, and when of bodily resurrection:

- *"What is rising?* In death, the separation of the soul from the body, the human body decays and the soul goes to meet God, while awaiting its reunion with its glorified body. God in his almighty power will definitively grant incorruptible life to our bodies by reuniting them with our souls, through the power of Jesus' resurrection.
- *Who will rise?* All the dead will rise: those who have done good to the resurrection of life, and those who have done evil to the resurrection of judgment.
- *How?* "How"exceeds our imagination and understanding; it is accessible only to faith.
- *When?* Definitively 'at the last day,' when history and the world as we know it ends. Indeed, the resurrection of the dead is closely associated with Christ's Parousia" (*Catechism* 997; 998; 1000; 1001).

A GLORIFIED BODY

In his theology, the Jesuit theologian Karl Rahner maintained that the resurrection of the body and the transformation of the universe are to be understood together, as both of these are beyond imagination. We speak of the Omega Point and the Universal Christ. However, can we possibly imagine either of these? Even though we cannot imagine either of these events or envision how they actually happen, we certainly can conceive of them. If we can conceive of Jesus having a risen and glorified body, then we might be able to conclude that it is at least possible that the resurrection of our own body into a glorified body could occur someday. However, there can be no dress rehearsal for us during this part of the play of life. Unrehearsed, we will only be able to take our cues from Jesus.

Finally, we are told both in the scriptures and the Tradition of the church, that as followers of Christ, we actually should expect a bodily resurrection similar to Jesus. What was seen and given testimony to by the disciples was that after the crucifixion and death of Jesus, it was Jesus who was, in fact, seen, but that his body was radically transformed. The reality of 'seeing Jesus' could only be expressed by symbolic and metaphorical expression of what it meant for his transformed body to "rise from the dead" and to be subsequently seen. This implied that what was seen was certainly more than merely a revivified corpse. The resurrection of Jesus is not a historical reality, it is trans-historical. We have no other language to talk about resurrection of the body other than to talk in terms of first seeing a seed and then seeing a flower, first seeing an acorn and then seeing an oak, first seeing a fetus and then seeing an adult, or first seeing a caterpillar and then seeing a butterfly. There exists in the "seeing" of both, a sameness and yet a simultaneous radical body transformation. The point is that there is harmonious continuity as well as transformative change. But, it will be only in the experience of our own resurrected body that we will then know exactly what our new and glorified body will be like. For now, we can only speak metaphorically of our bodily resurrection, look to Jesus as our model and for our cues, and then must simply put our faith and trust in a loving God of surprises. We can only believe in the mighty power of Jesus' rising. After that it must be sufficient for us to say:

> "Beloved, we are God's children now; what we shall be has not yet been revealed. We do know that when it is revealed we shall be like him, for we shall see him as he is" (1 John 3:2).

Chapter Fourteen

Reading the Signs of the Times

"He said to them in reply, 'In the evening you say, 'tomorrow will be fair, for the sky is red; and in the morning, today will be stormy for the sky is red and threatening.' You know how to judge the appearance of the sky, but you cannot judge the signs of the times" (Matt. 16:2–3).

JESUS, THE SIGN AND SACRAMENT

In any play everyone needs to read the script, know their respective lines, and to follow the cues of the Director. As was stated previously, the Director in the play of life is the Holy Spirit who guides us in our respective life roles.

Jesus, as the way, the truth, and the life is the primordial sign for the ages and the Sacrament of the Kingdom of God. In the above text from the Gospel of Matthew, Jesus rebukes the Pharisees and Sadducees for being able to read the indications of the coming weather and pending storms, but not the indications of the coming Kingdom of God. He is critical of their inability to see not only the coming of the Kingdom, but also the Kingdom in their midst, present in Jesus himself, as well as the signs that he offered them in the manner of his profound teaching and mighty works and deeds.

We find elsewhere in the Gospel texts of Matthew another of Jesus' warnings about reading the signs of the times. In this instance, he uses the myth of Jonah being swallowed into the belly of the whale for three days and three nights as a sign of his own prefigurement to enter the abode of the dead prior to his resurrection. Concerning the producing of signs for the removal of any possible doubt, Jesus tells the scribes and Pharisees as well as us prophetically:

"An evil and unfaithful generation seeks a sign, but no sign will be given it except the sign of Jonah the prophet. Just as Jonah was in the belly of the

whale three days and three nights, so will the Son of Man be in the heart of the
earth three days and three nights" (Matt. 12:39–40).

What greater sign do we have than the shadow of the cross and the ensuing
resurrection of Jesus from the dead, just as he had foretold. In addition,
through the Holy Spirit, God has been and is still at work in human history
and invites all of us to participate in that work. Seeing the historical action of
God and then discerning an appropriate response is what can be referred to
today as the definition of "reading the signs of the times." There are principal
characteristics of this age and a spiritual evolution that is emerging from the
collective consciousness of the people of God within the human community.
This can result in shared understandings and cooperative responses to what is
going on in the world.

Furthermore, we are also cautioned not to simply trust religious leaders to
read the signs for us as passive participants. The Gospels tell us clearly that
they can often overlook what is right under their noses. In reading the signs
of the times for ourselves, we can also slight or overlook the signs which God
has chosen as we seek signs of our own choosing and design. So it is always
best to discern in community what God might be saying to others among the
people of God.

Prior to the Second Coming of Christ, many more swirling storms will be
coming in the days ahead; we need to ready ourselves to read the warning
signs to interpret their meaning. We need to prepare ourselves to listen to
what the Holy Spirit is trying to tell us both personally and in community
with the people of God. The signs of God's work in the historical process are
not only occurring in our churches each Sunday morning. After all, Vatican
II has called us all to be "the Church in the Modern World." This of course, is
very different than being "the Church of the Modern World."

VATICAN II AND THE SIGNS OF THE TIMES

Since the end of Vatican Council II in 1965, Catholics, in particular, have
been repeatedly called to look for and attempt to comprehend the "signs of
the times." That particular key phrase has also been in almost every papal
encyclical which followed since 1965. The phrase was taken from several
scriptural references that speak to it and it was discussed in the council
document, *Pastoral Constitution on the Church*, also referred to as *Gaudium
Et Spes*. Here is what it stated:

> "To carry out such a task, the Church has always had the duty of scrutinizing
> the signs of the times and of interpreting them in the light of the Gospel. Thus,
> in language intelligible to each generation, she can respond to the perennial
> questions which men ask about this present life and the life to come and about

the relationship of the one to the other. We must therefore recognize and understand the world in which we live, its explanations, its longings, and its often dramatic characteristics" (Vatican Council II, Intro. Statement; IV)

"The People of God believes that it is led by the Lord's Spirit, who fills the earth. Motivated by this faith, it labors to decipher authentic signs of God's presence and purpose in the happenings, needs and desires in which this People has a part along with other men of our age" (Vatican Council II, Sec. I:XI).

THE CHURCH IN THE MODERN WORLD AND SIGNS

As people of God, we should be listening to and learning from the world around us. Since the time of Ignatius of Loyola, its founder, the Jesuit motto has been, *Finding God in all Things*. The motto declares that we certainly are in the world, though we don't necessarily have to be of the world. We will need to begin to cultivate a mature faith in order to be able to read the signs given us today and those which will be coming upon the earth. In many ways, the Vatican Council documents were a reiteration of some of the things that Jesus had been trying to prepare us for in the scriptures. For example:

"There will be signs in the sun, the moon, and the stars, and on earth, nations will be in disarray, perplexed by the roaring of the sea and the waves. People will die of fright in anticipation of what is coming upon the world, for the powers of the heavens will be shaken. And then they will see the Son of Man coming in a cloud with power and great glory. But when these signs begin to happen, stand erect and raise your heads because your redemption is at hand" (Luke 21:25–28).

With the first coming of Jesus Christ thousands of years ago, the days of our redemption were initiated. So, we can either focus on the fear which the above words could certainly elicit, or we can focus on standing erect and raising our heads as Jesus asked of us. Both the scriptures and Vatican II have issued the call for the latter in order that our hearts will be strengthened, we will take courage, and our fears will not get the better of us. This is why the most oft repeated statement in the scriptures, when God first speaks to us is, "Do not be afraid" or "Have no fear." The Lord speaks these words of comfort to us over 100 times throughout the entire Bible (Exod. Matt.14:27; Mark 6:50; Luke 5:10; John 6:20).

Prior to the Second Coming of Christ, we must begin to look at the signs on earth and those in the cosmos, in an attempt to discern and read their significance. And, we are not called simply to read the signs, but to discern their significance in the light of the Gospel message and only then to act. Pope John XXIII had told us after Vatican II, that the best way to interact with the signs of the times was to "see, judge, and act." Certain key world-wide events, occurrences, developing trends, societal, political, and institutional disintegration, and natural or cosmic disturbances should be a call for early vigilance. Much seems to have occurred in that regard in the modern world already.

The environment around us is crying out to us; climate change is just the tip of the iceberg. The seas are not necessarily roaring as yet, but the water levels are certainly changing; more floods in some areas; more draught in others; heavier rainstorms; record snowfalls. There seems to be far more earthquakes, tsunamis, hurricanes, and volcanic eruptions than there were several years ago. Wars and famines continue to plague us. We don't have to look too far to find cosmic disturbances, moral depravity, and nations in disarray. The signs are evident. But these are all part of the beginning stages and not the end of the end of the world as yet. The beginning of the end started with Jesus of Nazareth. What we are seeing around us currently, I believe, is symptomatic rather than full blown signs of a disease. Call them beginning symptoms or call them early warning signs, we are all looking at the same things, though we may be reading them and interpreting them differently than others as to their import.

POPE FRANCIS ON READING THE SIGNS OF THE TIMES

The spirit of the world wants us to have a single, uniform thought rather than the God given freedom to discern through the Spirit. Only praying to the Holy Spirit to give us the capacity to try to understand the signs of the times will empower us to be able to so. It is a beautiful thing to ask the Holy Spirit to direct us and for God to provide the grace.

This was part of the reflection on the Gospel that Pope Francis offered during his homily at Casa Santa Marta in November, 2013. Preaching on Christ's call to "read the signs of the times," the Holy Father told those present that we are all called to discern the passing of God through history. He further stated that in order to do this, we must think with our mind, heart and soul. In his homily, the Holy Father encouraged listeners with the following words:

> "The Lord wants us to understand what is happening: what is happening in my heart, what is happening in my life, what is happening in the world, in history . . . What is the meaning of what is happening now? . . . These are the signs of the times!" (Pope Francis; *Homily at Casa Santa Marta*).

In December, 2014, when speaking to the international group of theologians that advises him, Pope Francis asked them to respect a diversity of theological views and to listen to the "signs of the times" in their work. The Holy Father told them:

"Along with the entire Christian people, the theologian opens his eyes and ears to the 'signs of the times.'" The pope continued, quoting the Second Vatican Council document *Gaudium et Spes,*: "The theologian is called to 'hear, distinguish and interpret the many voices of our time, and judge them in the light of the word of God" (Pope Francis, *Address to Vatican Theological Commission*).

In his recent encyclical, *The Joy of the Gospel*, Pope Francis presented a rather lengthy Apostolic Exhortation in five chapters. In the opening sections of the second chapter, *"Amid the Crisis of Communal Commitment,"* Francis, quoting Paul VI, exhorts all communities to an "ever watchful scrutiny of the signs of the times." As he concludes the same chapter, he speaks of our attempt "to read the signs of the times."

As I prepared to finalize this book and get it ready for publication, Pope Francis had just convened a Vatican conference on climate change. The conference was called, *Protect the Earth; Dignify Humanity.* It included scientists, government officials, and religious leaders from around the world who have been attempting to read the signs of the times.

The conference was focused on the degree that climate change might be influenced by human causation and its resultant effect on world economics. It was reported that following this conference, the Holy Father would prepare an encyclical on the environment and human nature. It would attempt to show the inter-relationship between poverty, economic development, and climate change. More recently, the Papal Encyclical *Laudato Si* was published on May 24, 2015 and has certainly caused quite a stir within the Catholic Church and without. It broke new ground and is the first encyclical of its type written by any Pope.

Many believed that the Pope had no business delving into economic matters. However, "economics," from the Greek, *oikonomos,* is literally translated as "managing a home" or "household manager." The encyclical, *Laudato Si,* is therefore presented, as economics for the world we hold in common. It showcases the primacy of the common good over private property as outlined in Catholic Social Teaching since the time of Augustine. Here, the environment is seen as a common good with the poorest of the poor being the first to suffer most of the environment's upheavels. The encyclical calls for prayer, repentance, and an ongoing dialogue. These are initial steps which are seen as a potential remedy when something is drastically wrong with any household as perceived by the *oikonomos.* The Holy Father is merely playing his part in his role as a humble and concerned household manager.

Pursuant to his election, Pope Francis was the first pope in many years who was not actually present during Vatican Council II. Five popes before him did take an active role in the Council: John XXIII, Paul VI, John Paul I, John Paul II, and Benedict XVI. Their encyclicals were filled with language that encouraged the people of God to read the signs. However, the Holy Father, Pope Francis, has shown through his writing of both, *The Joy of The Gospel* and *Laudato Si* that he is filled with the same Council spirit and perspectives and expresses a most keen interest in the people of God being attuned to reading the signs of the times.

Finally, in Pope Francis' recent 53 minute address before both houses of the congress of the United States in Washington, D.C. on September 24, 2015, much of what the Holy Father had to say made reference to people in America reading the signs of the times not only as they relate to religious issues, but economic, political, and environmental issues as well. His address was consonant with the entire body of Catholic Social Teaching which was put forth by all of his predecessors with one of the common threads being "People before things." As we move toward the Omega Point of history, just as the Holy Father has his significant role being played out on the world stage, we all have our own smaller roles to act out as well. It is one of the many roles of the Holy Spirit to direct us in this play of life. The only way we can be sure of our small part in all of this is by trying to follow the script by reading the signs of the times.

Chapter Fifteen

The Omega Point

The Omega Point is the final act of the play of life. As the curtain rises, the scene opens with the Second Coming of Christ.

THE UNIVERSAL CHRIST

The Universal Christ can best be described as that aspect of God which "fills the universe and all its parts," as we are told in Ephesians 1:23. When we speak of the Universal Christ, it is meant first to imply the limitlessness of Christ in relation to time and space and that Christ does not belong any longer to any one particular age, any one particular nation, any one particular religion, or any one world. He is resurrected and vested with universal authority and has a universal mission. Furthermore, it implies that the life, death, and resurrection of Jesus is of the utmost significance to the entire universe which has now become Christocentric and has Christ as its center. Jesus of Nazareth, as a historical human being, is a matter of historical record. The Universal Christ who is risen, is more a matter of meaning and interpretation. Only the death of Jesus was an historical event; the resurrection, however, can be seen as only trans-historical as it impacts all of history, past, present, and future.

All of history is in movement and believed to be spiritually evolving toward Christ at the Omega Point. This will be the point at which the end of time and history as we know it is concluded and Christ will be God in all. Toward the end of their lives on this earth, both Jesuit theologians, Teilhard de Chardin and Karl Rahner, were attempting to develop a truly systematic theology of the risen Christ in relation to the evolving universe. Both sought to additionally provide proofs of the reality of the resurrection from more than appearance and empty tomb stories. In developing their theologies, both maintained that, in order to accomplish this work, one could not simply affirm the Universal Christ without affirming Jesus of Nazareth, the historical Jesus who died on the cross. To do this would make the risen Christ only some distorted cosmic idea or mythical icon. Teilhard de Chardin would write:

> "The mystical Christ, the Universal Christ of St. Paul has neither meaning nor value in our eyes except as an expansion of the Christ who was born of Mary and who died on the cross" (de Chardin, *Divine Milieu,* 89).

If the word "catholic" generally means "universal," where this is of particular importance to us as either Catholic or catholic, (small c), is when we envision the Universal Christ as the head of his body and we, in the Christian churches, as the Apostle Paul describes, as "the body of Christ" (1 Cor. 12:27). The import of this has both universal and personal impact. Each of us participates in a collective consciousness of the Universal Christ if our minds and hearts seek to be aligned with the mind and heart of Christ as the head of his body. It is the Holy Spirit of God within us as children of God who proceeds from the Father and the Son and seeks to unite us with the Universal Christ. It is this same Spirit who can direct us and point the way to the Universal Christ who, in his rising, is drawing all of us to the Omega Point.

CHRISTOLOGY/MODELS OF CHRIST

At the beginning of the Gospel of John, he tells us:

> "In the beginning was the Word, and the Word was with God, and the Word was God" (John 1:1).

The evangelist makes an opening statement here in his Gospel concerning the pre-existence of Jesus Christ, the incarnate Logos. In describing Jesus as Logos, he is also stating that Jesus is God's dynamic Word, personified pre-existent wisdom, the instrument of God's creative activity, and the summation of all intelligible reality.

So, the historical Jesus was seen by many in the early Christian community as the Incarnation of the Logos, henceforth known as the Universal Christ.

In most Theology classes taught at the University level, there have been two models of Christ that are usually presented. These models of Christ are called "Christology." They attempt to get at the nature, person, ministry, mission, and consciousness of Jesus Christ. In traditional Christology, there is seen to be the model of the "Christ from Above" and the model of the "Christ from Below."

The "Christ from Above" is the older of the two models. It speculates that Jesus came into this world from heaven with the full knowledge of who he was as the Christ. It begins with the Logos/the Word of God and does not negate the humanity of Jesus, but stresses his divinity. The "Christ from Below" model considers that Jesus slowly grew into his understanding of who he was and is as the Christ. It begins with the human Jesus of history and does not negate his divinity, but stresses his humanity.

Teilhard de Chardin S.J., was working toward presenting another model, the "Christ Ahead," model, who as Omega, was drawing a converging universe unto its end point; the Omega Point. He was developing this model, while at the same time clinging to the historical Jesus as the great revelation of God that stands behind all this. The "Christ Ahead," model neither negated nor diminished the "Christ Above," or the "Christ Below" models of Christ. The "Christ Ahead" model at the Omega Point however, was seen to be identical with the Universal Christ. Toward the end of his life, the modern Jesuit theologian Karl Rahner S.J. also wrote considerably on the "Christ Ahead" model, in his attempt to show the relationship between the resurrection of Christ and the transformation of the universe (Rahner, *Theological Investigations*, T.I. 21: 227, 252).

As well as being the Alpha, Jesus Christ is and always will be the Omega. The Omega Point however, is a particular term coined and developed by Teilhard de Chardin, French Jesuit priest, paleontologist, and Catholic theologian who wrote about it primarily in the early to mid-1900's. He died in 1955. Teilhard used the term to describe the purported maximum level of complexity and consciousness towards which the universe may be evolving. More specifically, it is posited as an end point toward which consciousness and evolution were converging. At the Omega Point the cosmos and consciousness are seen to converge upon the Universal Christ as God becomes all in all. Teilhard's basic premise was that all of reality, the whole of the cosmic order, is converging and spiritually evolving as it moves toward a final goal. It will be at the Omega Point that the universal becomes most personal. All of history is therefore in movement toward the Universal Christ and yet Christ is already present in the world. It is this presence of Christ as well as the person of Christ which now gives all of reality a Christic dimension and makes the universe Christocentric.

In his best known classic work, *The Phenomenon of Man*, Teilhard reconciled his religious faith with his academic interests as a paleontologist. He sought to combine Christian thought and theology with modern science and traditional philosophy. The book was finished in the 1930s, but was published posthumously in 1955. In the book, Teilhard set forth a sweeping account of the unfolding of the cosmos and the evolution of matter to humanity to ultimately a future reunion with the Universal Christ. Drawing from the works of early church fathers such as St. Ambrose and St. Augustine, Teilhard de Chardin abandoned literal interpretations of creation in the biblical Book of Genesis in favor of more allegorical and theological interpretations. He writes of the unfolding of the material cosmos, from primordial particles to the development of life and the evolution of the human being. He placed a much heavier emphasis on the spiritual evolution of humankind as opposed to the material evolution of humankind. Teilhard argued that the appearance of man brought an added dimension into the world. This he defines as the birth of reflection: animals know, but only man 'knows that he knows.'

ATTRIBUTES OF THE OMEGA POINT

In *The Phenomenon of Man*, Teilhard would write that the Omega point must possess the following four attributes . . . It is:

Actual:

It is already existing. Only thus can the rise of the universe towards higher stages of consciousness be explained. It is also personal, as it is an intellectual being and not an abstract idea. The increasing complexity of matter has not only led to higher forms of consciousness, but accordingly to more personalization, of which human beings are the highest attained form in the known universe. What is most personal is most universal and what is most universal is most personal. They are completely individualized, free centers of operation. It is in this way that man is said to be made in the image of God, who is the highest form of all personality. Teilhard expressly stated that at the Omega Point, when the universe becomes One, human persons will not be suppressed, but super-personalized.

The Jesuit theologian, Karl Rahner, who often referred to Teilhard in his writings, would later refer to this as the "supernatural existential." Personality will be infinitely enriched. This is because the Omega Point unites creation, and the more it unites creation, the increasing complexity of the universe aids in higher levels of consciousness. Thus, as God, the Creator creates, the universe evolves towards higher forms of complexity, consciousness, and finally with humans, personality, because God, who is drawing the universe towards Himself, is the most personal and universal of Beings.

Transcendent:

To be transcendent is to be beyond the limits of normal human experience. The Omega Point is not an "add on" and cannot be the result of the universe's final complex stage of its own consciousness. Instead, the Omega Point must exist even before the universe's evolution, because it is responsible for the rise of the universe toward more complexity, consciousness and personality.

This end point is outside the framework in which the universe rises because it is by its attraction that the universe evolves towards the supreme end point who is the Universal Christ.

Autonomous:

That is, free from the limitations of space and time. These are limits of a known universe of which God and God's Holy Spirit cannot be contained. The Omega Point is dynamic and moving without outside control or interference; God is not bounded by universal laws which are part of the universe which was created by God. God, being Holy Mystery, "Wholly Other," is more unknown than known. God is a transcendent reality; therefore, the Omega point can only be autonomous and free of universal limits.

Irreversible:

That is, attainable and imperative; it is inevitable. The process of spiritual evolution and the eventual convergence of a Christ consciousness at the Omega point at the end of time and history has already been set in motion. It began with the death and resurrection of Jesus Christ and the procession of the Holy Spirit. Following the Second Coming of Christ, convergence at the Omega Point must happen and cannot be undone or reversed. It is irreversible (de Chardin, *Phenomenon of Man*, 271).

EMERGING CHRIST CONSCIOUSNESS

As we are being pulled toward the Omega point, the whole of the historical process is in dynamic movement from lower to higher, from unconsciousness to consciousness, from consciousness to self-consciousness and then ultimately from self-consciousness to Christ-consciousness.

In this hypothesis of evolution in Teilhard's book, *The Future of Man* (1950), the universe is constantly developing towards higher levels of material complexity and consciousness. The evolving collective consciousness of humanity . . . the collective networks of thought and emotion in which all are immersed . . . Teilhard would describe as, 'the noosphere.' He would view this as a thinking layer that envelops the earth. The ultimate emergence of thought on earth and the ultimate pole of consciousness and complexity would be the Omega Point. In describing 'the noosphere' Teilhard would write:

> "A glow ripples outward from the first spark of conscious reflection. The point of ignition grows larger. The fire spreads in ever widening circles till finally the whole planet is covered with incandescence. Only one interpretation, only

one name can be found worthy of this grand phenomenon. Much more coherent and just as extensive as any preceding layer, it is really a new layer, the 'thinking layer' . . . In other words, outside and above the biosphere there is the noosphere . . . The earth 'gets a new skin'. Better still, it finds its soul" (de Chardin, *Phenomenon of Man*, 182–183).

THE OMEGA POINT: IDENTICAL WITH THE COSMIC CHRIST

Life as a play is continually in movement. All reality is dynamic and not static. The universe and all that is in it is in constant motion. For Teilhard, the universe can only be in motion and move in the direction of more complexity and consciousness if it is being drawn by a supreme point of complexity and consciousness. Thus Teilhard theorizes that the Omega Point as this supreme end point, is the actual cause for the universe to grow in complexity and consciousness.

Every play has a climax. The climactic moment in the play of life began with Jesus Christ. In other words, the Omega Point exists as supremely complex and conscious, transcendent and is independent of the evolving universe. Ultimately, as it evolves, the physical cosmos and the noosphere will begin to drive each other toward a climax. This resulting climax, is thus called the Omega Point. On the other hand, Teilhard believed that the Omega Point should not necessarily be viewed as something imminent. We can know almost nothing at this stage because Omega might not be reached for hundreds of thousands, or even millions of years.

Teilhard argued that the Omega Point resembles the Christian Logos, namely the Universal Christ, who draws all things unto himself. In the words of the Nicene Creed, Christ is "God from God," "Light from Light," "True God from true God," and "through him all things were made." Teilhard would write, "Christ is perfectly comparable to the Omega Point" (de Chardin, *Le Christique*, 7) and elsewhere, "Christ is identical with Omega" (de Chardin, *Science and Christ,* 54).

Teilhard saw this end point as a point of convergence, as the place where both the physical and "spiritual" (consciousness) would unite in an eschatological event. This place is where the cosmos meets God in the Cosmic Christ. Our destiny, therefore, is interwoven with the destiny of Christ and all our destinies will ultimately converge with the Universal Christ. It is God, in Christ, within us, in the dynamism of the Holy Spirit, who is the principal and power of our self-transcendence and the universal force propelling us toward this meeting point.

It is also the mysterious capacity within the human person to become a higher being with greater consciousness while remaining at all times thoroughly human. Through the dynamism of the Holy Spirit within us and the acceptance of grace, we can orient ourselves to the Universal Christ who is the transcendent ground of all universal reality and is moving with us toward this end point. From this universal center even now at our place and time in history, there is emanating a radiation which prior to the death and resurrection of Jesus Christ had been perceptible only to those persons who were called mystics. Teilhard would write:

> "But Omega, as we have seen is not merely the name for collective reflection at the end of time. It is also and more fundamentally the name for that supreme personal Being here and now responsible for the process itself . . . the real Omega, the Prime Mover ahead . . . who not only is, but has always been. If therefore, the Christ of revelation, is to be identified with the omega of evolution, (this is TDC's initial supposition) then that which is responsible for relating the Parousia to mankind's planetary maturation must somehow already be present in the life, death, and resurrection of Jesus of Nazareth. In the person of Jesus, the real Omega took flesh and became part of that evolutionary current for which he himself is responsible" (Mooney, 63).

THE EVOLUTION OF THE SPIRIT

Teilhard saw the process of evolution as a sequence of progressive syntheses whose ultimate convergence point is that of God. As human persons we are situated in time and space as well as history. As such, we are both historical and transcendental creatures. We evolve by opening ourselves to God who unites all of creation. Our self-transcending in response to God's call and the accepting of grace allows for our spiritual evolution. When humanity and the material world have reached their final state of evolution and exhausted all potential for further development, a new convergence between them and the supernatural order would be initiated by the Second Coming of Christ. Teilhard asserted that the work of Christ is primarily to lead the material world to this cosmic redemption.

Finally, he moves to a description of his vision of the Omega Point as supreme consciousness in the future, which is "pulling" all creation towards it. He makes sense of the universe by its evolutionary process. He believed that spiritual development is moved by the same universal laws as material development and that it is evolving. If nature's goal is spirit, then the cosmos is related to its ground or source. He maintained that evolution requires a unification of consciousness. As such, it was "an ascent toward consciousness." It therefore, signifies a continuous upsurge toward the Omega Point who is the Universal Christ, who is God. On this matter, Teilhard would write:

> "It is under the illuminative influence of grace that our mind recognizes in the unitive character of the Christian phenomenon a manifestation (reflection) of Omega upon the human consciousness and it identifies the omega of reason

with the Universal Christ of revelation" (de Chardin, *The Heart of Matter,* 144).

FINDING GOD IN ALL THINGS

Vatican Council II has called us to be "the Church in the Modern World." In his second comprehensive work, *The Divine Milieu*, Teilhard attempted to reverse the 19th and early 20th century belief among some Catholics and other Christians that in order to be "holy" one had to devote oneself to purely religious activity and that secular work had no lasting value. As a Jesuit, Teilhard de Chardin believed in the Ignation motto, "Find God in all things." He wanted to demonstrate that secular work (including his own scientific work) was an integral part of creation and the Incarnation, so that for religious reasons, Christians should be committed to whatever work they were doing in the world and to offer it up for the service of God. Teilhard wanted to show how all human activities and efforts toward personal growth and human progress can be used to help the growth and development of the Body of Christ and that in doing this, we are many different members, but one body. To Teilhard, the highest stage of material development is life, and the highest stage in the development of life is a human life. Not only are all human efforts and activities beneficial in regard to our relatedness to the world, but they are also somehow very necessary.

We should envision the world as more than simply the earth, for it is more; it is the "Divine Mileau." Even though people perform these actions as ordinary human beings in the workaday world, and they look like ordinary human actions, they are simultaneously being divinized and transformed in the divine milieu. As such, they become actions done in, with, and through cooperation with the Universal Christ as we move in the direction of the Omega Point. Teilhard would write:

> "God reveals himself everywhere, beneath our groping efforts, as a universal mileau, only because he is the ultimate point upon which all realities converge.
> " also "The earth has become for me, over and above herself, the body of him who is and of him who is coming" (de Chardin, *The Divine Mileau*, 85, 134).

Like St Francis of Assisi before him, Teilhard saw the principle of sacramentality at work in creation and all creatures. He found the presence of God everywhere and in everything in the universe around him.

POINTING THE WAY TO OMEGA

How is it possible that all evolved consciousness and complexity in the cosmos could one day meet somehow at the Omega Point who is the Universal Christ as God becomes all in all? In reality, everyone is looking for God. As Augustine said, "Our hearts are restless until they rest in thee." It is necessary that those of us who have experienced God's grace and received the indwelling Holy Spirit, should try to help others find the way. As Christian evangelists, we should lead by example, make sacrifices, and share the gospel at the proper time with family, friends, and acquaintances. As Catholics in particular, we should truly attempt to live out the spirit of Vatican II as a church in the world, but not of the world. We should be taking the church with us out into the corporations we work in, the grocery stores we shop in, the cocktail parties, tennis matches, pool parties, or friendly gatherings etc., we participate in. For this is where we live most of our lives, we don't live our lives in the church building except on Sunday mornings. When we act with love in ways large and small wherever we are, we touch the lives of others with God's Spirit.

As has been stated previously, Teilhard maintained that in terms of the development of our consciousness, we should continually be moving from unconsciousness to consciousness to self-consciousness to Christ-consciousness. It is this Christ consciousness which occurs in its entirety at this final stage of consciousness. Human spiritual development is dynamic, is moving and being moved by the same universal laws as material development. This implies, of course, that there exists at the Omega Point already, a Prime Mover of the Spirit, the Universal Christ, who is drawing us toward our ultimate destiny. And it is the Holy Spirit within us that directs and empowers us to draw others along with us to Omega. The Holy Spirit always points toward Christ. This Christ consciousness will continue to spiritually evolve now and in the future and ultimately be drawn toward the Omega Point at the end of time and history as we know it. It will be at the Omega Point where all consciousness will converge as God in the Universal Christ, becomes all in all. At that point, in the final act of the play of life, all loose ends will come together as we experience a denouement. The plot of the play will thicken and then suddenly become clear to all of us as we move finally and completely into and converge ultimately with the Spirit of the Universal Christ.

For, we will then be One in the Spirit; God in us, us in God. Paul tells us in 1st Corinthians and the Letter to the Ephesians:

> "Whoever is joined to the Lord becomes One Spirit with him . . . Do you not know that your body is a temple of the Holy Spirit within you, whom you have from God and that you are not your own?" (1 Cor. 6:17, 19) And

> "In Him you also are being built together into a dwelling place for God in the Spirit" (Eph. 2:22).

Chapter Sixteen

Self-Transcendence and the Omega Point

SELF-REALIZATION

In the play of life all energy is dynamically moving from the beginning of life and being drawn toward its end at the Omega Point as God becomes all in all. Self-Realization is a realizing of oneself in the dynamism of ongoing life. It is the transition of a life from potentiality to reality. As Christians we believe that The Holy Spirit within us is the principle and power of our self-realizing (as well as the principle and power of self-transcendence). Self-realization begins for us with an acceptance of grace. It cannot be equated with any kind of intellectual knowledge and does not occur as a process of rational thought. It is spiritual awareness and consciousness that is realized apart from our intellectually knowing it; it is consciousness without knowledge. The true self begins to emerge in Christ. Because there is freedom and choice involved by virtue of our humanity, self-realization can become self-refusal. Our acceptance of grace allows the Holy Spirit to essentially realize our being in God. We do not essentially realize God being in us because there is consciousness without our knowledge of it.

THEOLOGY OF SELF-TRANSCENDENCE

The word, "transcendence," can be defined as "surpassing the limits of ordinary experience." Its etymology is from the Latin, "trans" meaning "beyond" and "scandare" which means "to climb." So literally it means "climbing beyond." As stated previously, human beings are both transcendental and historical creatures. We have the potential to be more than who we are as a "self," transcending and spiritually evolving while in communion with God.

Christian thinkers after St. Augustine recognized that the human person has an "inner" transcendence. We are spiritual beings in communion with God. The spirit has in its being a genuine relation to the Absolute. We evolve by opening ourselves to God who unites all creation. Our goal as human beings should be to become our true selves as we encounter God in the cosmos.

Any Christian theology of self-transcendence should be grounded in God in Christ as both the self-communication of God and the object of our active self-transcending. It should also have the experiences of Christian prayer, spiritual reflection, and thoughtful meditation as a basis. God, in the Incarnation of Christ, became human so that he could encounter us as humans within the realm and confines of time and space in which we exist.

All of creation is united in its one origin in God and in its one future in God. Any historical and transcendental evolutionary process depends on its end already being in its beginning. Christ then became for us, not only the beginning of our experience of self-transcendence, but also the ultimate promise of the future fulfillment of God's self-communication at the Omega Point of history.

TRANSCENDENTAL ANTHROPOLOGY

The most prominent Catholic theologian of the 20th century, Karl Rahner S. J., believed that, as human beings, any experience we have of God is an experience of transcendence. His theology has been called, "transcendental anthropology." Rahner's starting point for this theology was always the human person, who is simultaneously an historical and transcendental being. He argued that theology and anthropology always go together; we can't say anything about God without also saying something about human beings, and vice versa. For example, when we say "God heard my prayer," we create the implication that God has ears like we do. As a theology, Transcendental Anthropology is centered on the belief that human openness to transcendence is founded in the pre-apprehension of the transcendent God. Thus, it is important for Rahner to caution his reader not to confuse human transcendence with God's transcendence. In his theological studies, Rahner also identified a need to develop the thought of Teilhard de Chardin with more precision and clarity. He believed that it should show the intelligible connection between Jesus of Nazareth and the resurrected Christ as the Omega point of world evolution. (Rahner, *Theological Investigations,* 21:227).

Also, in his *Foundations of Faith,* Karl Rahner talks a great deal about his theory of self-transcendence and a truer understanding of the relation between matter and spirit. Rahner says, "It is of the intrinsic nature of matter to develop toward spirit" In this context, he reflects on the transitions to the new in the history of the universe, particularly when matter becomes life, and when life becomes self-conscious spirit. Transcending ourselves by responding to God's call is a kind of spiritual evolution. As human beings, we are situated in space and time as well as in history. In time, a person can change; he or she develops. In this development, the person transcends his or her former self. Indeed, one surpasses oneself, and in the act of becoming, one actually "increases" one's own being. This is "active self-transcendence;" one transcends oneself. "The Theology of Self-Transcendence" could also easily be called the "Theology of Becoming." God's creative act should be understood not only as enabling the universe to exist as a static reality, but also as enabling it to become (Rahner, *Theological Investigations,* 21).

Rahner's concept of active self-transcendence recovers the notion of biological evolution as an on-going process where indeed something new emerges. Rahner states:

"The essence of any being whose self-transcendence is in question does not determine the limits of what can be produced in the advance beyond itself. It can, however, be an indication that from some definite limited potentiality, something is coming to be and must come about that is not yet a reality" (Rahner, "Hominization," Section 3).

Rahner sees the Christ-event as the definitive act of self-transcendence within the created universe. Transcendental self-communication is the action of God. The Christ-event is the apex of the self-transcendence of the evolving universe into God. Christ is God's complete offer of self-communication and the event has universal implications in that it is salvific for the whole of reality. Jesus is part of the process of the world's becoming that gives itself radically as the universe spiritually evolves into divine love. The ground of our being becomes the One toward whom the person is being drawn. It is a magnet which draws us to transcend what we were and to become what and who we are called to be. It is, in short, the work of God's Spirit and the acceptance of God's grace; we only cooperate with the Holy Spirit within us which points to the Universal Christ.

In the human being, as part of the process of active self-transcendence, the cosmos presses forward and evolves as it is reaching toward its own "self-presence in spirit" (Rahner *Foundations*, 183–190). The resurrection of Jesus Christ was the beginning of the transformation of the universe. As Christians, we are after all, part of the body of Christ and the universe as it is evolving is Christocentric. Therefore we are both part of the body of Christ and the evolving Christocentric universe:

"Now you are Christ's body, and individually parts of it." (1 Cor. 12:27)

ACTIVE SELF-TRANSCENDENCE

So, Christ is not only within us now in the Holy Spirit as we evolve as his body in active self-transcendence, but he also waits for us there at the Omega Point, at the end of time and history, in all his glorified body as the Universal Christ. As was stated earlier, The Universal Christ can best be described as that aspect of God which "fills the universe and all its parts," as we are told in Ephesians 1:23 or as the Christ of the Cosmos as described in the hymn found in Colossians, Chapter one:

> "He is the image of the invisible God, the firstborn of all creation. For in him were created all things in heaven and on earth, the visible and the invisible, whether thrones or dominations, principalities or powers; all things were created through him and for him. He is before all things, and in him all things hold together. He is the head of the body, the church. He is the beginning, the first born from the dead, that in all things he himself might be pre-eminent. For in him all the fullness was pleased to dwell, and through him to reconcile all things for him, making peace by the blood of his cross through him, whether those on earth or those in heaven" (Col. 1:15–20).

We creatures of the world find ourselves in the manner that God has given to us and that is the way of self-transcendence. Transcending ourselves in response to God's call and the acceptance of grace allows for our spiritual evolution. Therefore, as persons, we are not just a product of the cosmos, but our spiritual union with God and God's Spirit, The Holy Spirit, allows us to self-transcend. The Holy Spirit of God in us is the very ground and the goal of our being as we continue to become drawn toward the Omega point of the cosmos where God is drawing all of us, to meet with the Universal Christ who is all in all. Therefore, as part of the Second Coming of Christ (the Parousia), we are coming to Christ in as much as Christ is coming to us.

In active self-transcending, we attempt to synchronize our mind with the mind of Christ so that our thoughts might be identified with Christ's thoughts and our consciousness is evolving to become more Christ-Conscious. Our knowledge is developed through our faith in Christ and the power of his rising; it is not a matter of degree as much as a matter of essence. Our faith in Christ brings about a unification of our thinking with those who are and have been Christ-conscious.

As we actively self-transcend, because the risen Christ is already at the Omega Point, some of our Christ-centered thoughts will be future-thought and some of our knowledge, future-knowledge. Our future-knowing is not distinguished from our future-being, as active self-transcending as has been stated previously, is a theology of becoming. Matter and spirit within us as persons is not opposed or separate, but united. It is the nature of matter to develop toward spirit. In self-transcending we spiritually evolve, and as we gradually transcend the merely material, we begin to recognize it for what it is, namely, the vehicle of the spirit. All that is transcendent within us reaches out through grace to, "touch the cloak of God," who is Absolute Transcendence and the Holiest of Mysteries. Karl Rahner refers to this as the "supernatural existential" which he defines as follows:

> "The supernatural existential refers to God's free fulfillment of a human person's openness to being through God's "self-gift" of grace. We have been created from the very beginning for the grace of God's self- communication" (Rahner, *Foundations of Christian Faith*).

To Rahner, in discussing the supernatural existential, grace becomes a permanent modification of our human nature. In his description of this process, Teilhard de Chardin would similarly refer to this as the "transcendent superego." (de Chardin, *The Heart of Matter*, 39)

Because, through grace, we have the Holy Spirit within us, we can continue to ask humbly in faith; and through prayer and active contemplation, for some small sharing in the mind of the Universal Christ. God, in the presence and power of the Holy Spirit, takes possession of our spirit and draws us into the mystery. As we spiritually evolve, we are drawn deeper into the mystery, gradually transcending who we were as a self and becoming the self we are called to be.

Chapter Seventeen

The Rapture; a Catholic Perspective

THE WRITING OF THE BIBLE

Christian Fundamentalists believe in the literal interpretation of the Bible; "God said it, and I believe it. Period." This is not the best approach to the bible under all circumstances. The problem with taking a Fundamentalist approach to the Bible, is that everything we know about those who wrote the Bible, under the inspiration of the Holy Spirit, indicates that they did not want the bible understood in that manner each and every time. They wrote as being situated in a certain historical setting and as part of a particular culture. They sometimes wrote literally, but more often than not, they wrote using literary devices such as similes, metaphors, allegories, myths, parables, and apocryphal and other descriptive language. Many of these literary devices are often the language of the playwright as well.

Therefore, the best way to try to understand what the Biblical writers were trying to convey to us and what the Holy Spirit is saying, is through looking at the historical setting and context in which they wrote the words. Then, we should take a critical approach to those words in an attempt to arrive at the full meaning of the writer's words to determine what God might be saying.

Please understand, however, that this method does not negate the fact that the words should still be considered as the "Word of God" spoken through humankind. It merely negates a literal interpretation and Fundamentalist approach to the Bible in every instance as the intention of the writers. The Book of Genesis is a perfect example. The writers primarily used myth as their literary device and if we were to interpret the words literally, we would not comprehend the message they were trying to tell us. The same is true of the Book of Revelation which uses rich symbolism to convey its message. If we attempt to understand anything in the Book of Revelation without looking at the historical background that occasioned its writing, it would be impossible to grasp the meaning.

The Historical-Critical method is the method used by the Catholic Church to try to understand what the various writers of the Bible were trying to convey to us. It allows the reader to try to understand critically what any given writer in their historical setting and culture was saying. To give an example, using our language of today, if I were to write, "It's raining cats and dogs," I wouldn't want to convey the thought that felines and canines were literally falling from the skies. I would simply want to convey that it was raining very heavily.

Modern Catholic theologian, Bernard Lonergan, S.J. has said that what is necessary for both professional and everyday readers to truly understand the Bible is religious, moral, and intellectual conversion. Understanding the Bible concerns our eternity. Conversion turns us from being hearers of the Bible to doers, and from experts in interpretation to experts in hearing the voice of God in our everyday lives (Martens, 42).

At this juncture, I would like to discuss the Fundamentalist doctrine of the Rapture and attempt to give a Catholic perspective and theological understanding of the basis of this doctrine.

WHAT IS THE RAPTURE?

Throughout this book we have made reference to life as a play and been discussing many of the end times roles the actors and actresses have in this play of life. Human life is filled with drama. To reference William Shakespeare once again:

> "All the world's a stage and all the men and women merely players" (Shakespeare, *As You Like It,* Act II, Sc. VII).

However, any play that aims to entertain an audience through situations that are highly exaggerated, absurd, sensationalized, and overly dramatized can be called by its literary term, "a farce."

The doctrine of the Rapture was virtually unheard of prior to the 18th century. It is a relatively recent development made popular today by modern Christian Fundamentalists, such as Hal Lindsey (*The Late Great Planet Earth*), Tim LaHaye (*Bible Prophecy; the Left Behind series; The Beginning of the End*) and others. These type of books are long on spectacle and short on Biblical grounding as well as any trace of historical and valid theological investigation and evidence. They stretch Biblical truth into overt sensationalism and heightened drama.

The so-called, "Rapture," is a mysterious disappearance event of some of earth's people, who leave their clothes here on earth as they depart. Cars which were driven by the "saved" are left unpeopled in the middle of the road. People disappear from airplanes flying in the sky as well. The folks left behind are in a tizzy as to what happened. A great tribulation follows upon the earth, and the antichrist appears. The ones who are left behind then get a second chance at "being saved," if they can withstand the evil forces of the world-uniting and the antichrist. Ultimately, Jesus returns again to defeat the antichrist. This is more like Christianized science fiction than anything else. And none of this, except for the overall premise of a "rapture" in the letter from Paul to the Thessalonians is Biblically based. Why? The Bible says something very different will occur in the Book of Revelation:

"Behold, he is coming amid the clouds, and every eye will see him, even those who pierced him. All the peoples of the earth will lament him. Yes, Amen" (Rev. 1:7).

Fundamentalist and conservative Evangelical groups continue to grow vigorously, particularly in the Western world. Many of these Fundamentalists — including "born-again" Christians, "Bible-believing" Christians, "saved" Christians, "non-denominational" Christians, Pentecostal Christians, and other Fundamentalist church groups are very antagonistic toward the Catholic Church and her teachings which vigorously denies their value or contribution to authentic theological investigation. These groups often take one specific text of the Bible and make an entire doctrine or dogma from it. This certainly is the case with the doctrine of the Rapture.

The primary text which they cite which refers to the doctrine is 1 Thessalonians 4:15–17, which states:

"Indeed, we tell you this, on the word of the Lord, that we who are alive, who are left until the coming of the Lord, will surely not precede those who have fallen asleep. For the Lord himself, with a word of command, will descend from heaven with a cry of command, with the voice of an archangel, and with the trumpet of God, will come down from heaven, and the dead in Christ will rise first. Then we who are alive, who are left, will be caught up together with them in the clouds to meet the Lord in the air. Thus we shall always be with the Lord" (1 Th. 4:15–17).

According to this doctrine, when Christ returns at the Second Coming, all of the elect who have died will be raised and transformed into a state of glory, along with the living elect, and then be caught up to be with Christ in the clouds. The Latin verb which is used for "being caught up together" is "rapiemur," and it is from the use of this particular Latin verb that the name, "rapture," came to be.

A CATHOLIC'S UNDERSTANDING OF THE RAPTURE

With respect to the doctrine of the Rapture, Catholics certainly believe that the event of our gathering together to be with Christ will take place, although they do not generally use the word "rapture" to refer to this event or envision the event unfolding the way Fundamentalists view it. The so-called Rapture doctrine which Christian Fundamentalists hold to is also enmeshed in much confusion due to the varied positions held on what is referred to as "Millennialism." Because of this, much fiction and spectacle concerning the specific Thessalonians text has been mixed in with truth. This has blurred the lines between what has been revealed in scripture, and what are simply fanatical and way- out ideas. Some ultra-Fundamentalist thinkers have made this into kind of a "Left Behind" event. They view this event in a way that those who are right with God are mysteriously winged up into heaven, and those who are living in sin, remain on earth during a time of tribulation and chaos.

The Catholic teaching on the end times, however, does not support this type of thinking. One of the problems this understanding conveys is that there might be two "second comings" of Jesus. Once when the people mysteriously disappear, and then again when Jesus returns again and defeats the antichrist. The scripture tells us clearly that there will be one Second Coming of Christ. In verse 15, Paul says, "THE coming," not "A Coming" (1 Th. 4:15).

The Catholic understanding of the above 1 Thessalonians 4 text is that those believers who are alive during Christ's Second Coming will not experience death. Paul does indicate that the timing of this is unknown, although he seemingly expects it to occur during his lifetime. Those Christian believers will be gloriously transformed and then join the saints already with Christ. St. Paul states in the letter to the Thessalonians that Christ's coming will be announced by the cry of an archangel and by a trumpet blast. St. Paul is describing the resurrection of the dead that will take place at Christ's Second Coming. When reading 1 Thessalonians it appears that Christians at the time were worried that those who died before Christ's Second Coming would not share in His triumphant return. Paul assures them that when the time comes, they will join the resurrected to meet the Lord and will share in Christ's triumphant return.

Finally, the so-called Rapture is not an event whereby the faithful are removed from the world before a time of suffering and tribulation comes upon the earth. As Christ suffered, so also must the Church suffer which follows after him. The Great Tribulation is discussed in Matthew Chapter 24:1–31. We are told in the Catechism of the Catholic Church as well:

> "Before Christ's Second Coming, the church must pass through a final trial that will shake the faith of many believers. The persecution that accompanies

her pilgrimage on earth will unveil the 'mystery of iniquity' in the form of
religious deception offering humankind an apparent solution to their problems
at the price of apostasy from the truth" (*Catechism* 675).

So the question becomes . . . "Will something happen such as described in
1 Thessalonians 4:15–17?" The answer is clearly, YES! However, it will be a
one-time event, on the last day of our earthly existence, after the dead have
been raised, and it will be seen and witnessed by all and not a select few. So,
to buy into the doctrine of the Rapture as depicted by Christian Fundamentalists is to be misled by dramatized science fiction being promulgated as cred-
ible theology. It fails to recognize that it lacks any serious contribution to
theological investigation. In the language of the playwright, it is a "farce."

MILLENNIALISM AND THE RAPTURE

Millennialism (from "millennium," Latin for "thousand years") is a belief
held by some Christians that there will be a Golden Age or Paradise on Earth
in which "Christ will reign" for 1000 years prior to the final judgment and
future eternal state with the emergence of the New Heavens and New Earth.
This belief is derived primarily from The Book of Revelation 20:1–6:

> "Then I saw an angel come down from heaven, holding in his hand the key to
> the abyss and a heavy chain. He seized the dragon, the ancient serpent, which
> is the devil or Satan, and tied it up for a thousand years and threw it in the
> abyss, which he locked over it and sealed, so that it could no longer lead the
> nations astray until the thousand years are completed. After this, it is to be
> released for a short time. Then I saw thrones; those who sat on them were
> entrusted with judgment. I also saw the souls of those who had been beheaded
> for their witness to Jesus and for the word of God, and who had not wor-
> shipped the beast or its image nor had accepted its mark on their foreheads or
> hands. They came to life and reigned with Christ for a thousand years. The rest
> of the dead did not come to life until the thousand years were over. This is the
> first resurrection. Blessed and holy is the one who shares in the first resurrec-
> tion. The second death has no power over these; they will be priests of God
> and of Christ, and they will reign with him for the thousand years" (Rev.
> 20:1–6).

What makes this confusing is that Christians are split into three different
camps with three different takes on the Millennium. The three schools of
thought are called Post-millennialism, Pre-millennialism and A-millennial-
ism.

POST-MILLENNIALISM

Post-millennialism is the view of the last things which holds that the Kingdom of God is now being extended in the world through the preaching of the gospel to all the nations, and that through the saving work of the Holy Spirit, the world will eventually be totally Christianized. The return of Christ at the Second Coming will occur at the end of a long period of righteousness and peace on earth . . . that period being the Millennium.

Today only a very few ultra-conservative Protestant denominations hold to this view. Post-Millennialists have said that the Millennium spoken of in Revelation 20 should be understood figuratively. The phrase "a thousand years" refers not to a fixed period of ten centuries but only implies an indefinite long period of time.

In the Post-Millennial school of thought, the Millennium's end will usher in the Second Coming, the general resurrection of the dead, and the final judgment.

The major problem with the Post-Millennial viewpoint is that nowhere in Scripture does it depict the world as experiencing a period of complete Christianization before the Second Coming of Christ. This position is not Biblically based, but is the result of certain doctrines promulgated within the conservative element of the Protestant Tradition. In fact, there are numerous Biblical verses that say just the opposite. They speak of the age between the First and Second Comings of Christ as a time of great sorrow, pain, and tribulation for Christians. So without any Biblical evidence to support that the world will eventually become totally Christian before the Second Coming, one would have to conclude that the just and the wicked will probably populate the earth together until the final judgment.

PRE-MILLENNIALISM

Many more of our Protestant brothers and sisters take a Pre-Millennialist approach to the so-called Rapture. Most of the books written about the end times today take this approach. Like the Post-Millennialists, the Pre-Millennialists believe that there will be a thousand year reign where the earth will be thoroughly Christianized. One of the major differences, however, is that most Millennialists believe that this will occur after the Second Coming of Christ rather than before. According to them, the final judgment will occur after the Millennium period of a thousand years. In this view, it is believed that Christ will reign for a thousand years on earth during the Millennium. This theory gives the mistaken impression that there will seemingly be a third coming of Christ after the second coming of Christ. There is nothing in scripture, however, that supports the premise that a thousand years will separate the Second Coming of Christ and the final judgment.

A-MILLENNIALISM

The Catholic position has thus historically been, "A-Millennial," as has been the understanding of a majority of the Christian churches in general, including the Protestant Reformers in the 1500's. It should be noted, however, that Catholics do not typically use this term. It merely is a word to denote a position against other millennial positions. It is a rejection of the belief that Jesus will have a literal, thousand-year-long, physical reign on the earth. It takes the view that Revelation 20, because it is part of the Book of Revelation in the Bible, is written as "Apocrypha," and is intended to convey a symbolic meaning. This view perceives the Millennium not as an earthly golden age in which the world will be totally Christianized, but more as the present period of Christ's rule in heaven as well as on the earth through his Church.

The "1000 years" of Revelation 20:1–6 is a metaphorical reference to the present church age which will culminate in Christ's return at the Second Coming. Additionally, A-Millennialists believe that both good and evil will exist alongside each other until the end of time and Christ's Second Coming. Here we tend to agree with the church father, Augustine, and as such are not in agreement with either the Post-Millennial or Pre-Millennial positions.

Where most Christians can agree however, with many of our separated brothers and sisters in Christ is that Jesus Christ is Lord and will indeed come again in his glorified body at the Second Coming. This will end time and history as we know it and fully usher in the Kingdom of God and the Eternal Reign of God. Maranatha.

Chapter Eighteen

Anonymous Christians and Salvation

"He (Jesus Christ) is the stone rejected by you, the builders, which has become the cornerstone. There is no salvation through anyone else, nor is there any other name under heaven given to the human race by which we are to be saved" (Acts 4:11–12).

Unfortunately, the above text has often been used by Fundamentalist Christians and others to send all Hindus, Moslems, Buddhists, etc. to hell who have not professed belief in Christianity as a world religion and Jesus Christ as their personal Savior. But, when the Apostle Peter voiced those words in the first century of the Christian Church, the Roman world he lived in considered salvation to be in the hands of the emperor. It was the emperor who was often hailed as "savior" and a "god." Peter, before the Sanhedrin, is firmly denying that deliverance comes through anyone other than the risen Jesus and in his name. Furthermore, Peter is addressing his words to many Jewish Sadducees among the elders and leaders who don't believe in a bodily resurrection at all.

I maintain that Peter was certainly accurate with what he said and his statement is true of course; I do firmly believe it. However, that being said, I also believe that any and all salvation is more in the hands of Jesus Christ than any of our hands and the acceptance of salvation in Christ applies to more than our earthly professions in words of faith. I also believe that the Holy Spirit can work through all the good that may be found in other World Religions and that God's Providence can work through any and all human error. We simply cannot put the Holy Spirit in a box.

In the past century, particularly since Vatican Council II, many in the Catholic Church have moved from an exclusive to an inclusive view regarding Christ and the salvation of non-Christians. Therefore, along with several other Catholic theologians, teachers of the Catholic faith, and Catholic writers, I maintain that no salvation can be had apart from Jesus Christ. However, it is only through the grace of God that there can be such a thing which Vatican Council II theology has called an "anonymous Christian."

WHAT IS AN ANONYMOUS CHRISTIAN?

Any major play has "supporting actors and actresses," but to many the topic of anonymous Christians will seem slightly "off script." An anonymous Christian is not a professed or explicit Christian. It is one who is living out the gospel message of Jesus Christ without recognizing it as such. They are aligned with Christ, the Christian church and its Tradition, but have not been ritually baptized into Christianity. They could be viewed as fragmented parts of a whole that have the possibility of salvation through the Universal Christ. They are seeking Jesus Christ, even though they wouldn't know that and use that language or ever call themselves anonymous Christians. Their relationship to Christ is different, of course, than one who professes and believes that Jesus is Lord and Savior. Furthermore, we would never insult them by calling them by the term "anonymous Christian," any more than they would address us as anonymous Buddhists, Hindus, or Jews. When we use the term "anonymous Christian" we are speaking of someone who acts out their life in Christian love and who has at least the possibility of salvation through the Universal Christ at the Omega Point of history. For even when we use the words, "Universal Christ," we are speaking of something beyond Christianity as a world religion and which surpasses our powers of reason and logic. To quote St. Theresa of Avila, a Doctor of the Church:

"God surpasses reason in bestowing consolation . . ." (Theresa of Avila).

For an anonymous Christian, the light of Christ is probably shining in the darkness of the universe, though the light appears distant to them and the cloud has not lifted as yet. Rabbi Abraham Heschel, who was invited to represent the Jewish Religion at Vatican Council II, was the most prominent Jewish theologian of our time and one whom some might consider to have been an anonymous Christian. I believe that he may have said as much in his own words even though he would never state that he was an anonymous Christian. Rabbi Heschel wrote:

"God is not a hypothesis derived from logical assumptions, but an immediate insight, self-evident as light. He is not something to be sought in the darkness with the light of reason. He is the light" (Heschel, 337).

The light will continue to draw all to it who truly believe, as does Rabbi Heschel, that "*God is in Search of Man* while man is seeking God." But, the

God of the universe dwells in unapproachable light, so brilliant that it blinds the searching eye and burns the questioning mind that seeks answers found in the light of reason. Yet to the Christian, God took on a human face and form in Jesus of Nazareth; God from God; light from light.

Until the end of history as we know it, Christ the light will continue to shine in the darkness that has not overcome it (John 1:5). And I believe that Rabbi Heschel, an anonymous Christian, will rise one day to come before the Universal Christ; who is the God of the universe and the light of the world who will dawn in the darkness.

Let me state at this juncture once more, that I certainly believe that there is no salvation outside of Jesus Christ and that no one can "come to the Father" except through Him. There should be no question here of what I believe. From there, I'd like to discuss what might be possible when so called, 'anonymous Christians,' meet the Universal Christ at the Omega point.

Ever since his election as Pope on March 13, 2013, Pope Francis has often been called, "the Pope of Mercy." In fact, as has been stated earlier, he has declared from December 2015 to November 2016 to be a "Jubilee Year of Mercy." As Pope, he has also frequently proclaimed to the world the God of Mercy who wants to save people, not condemn them. He has voiced this in several of his homilies:

> "The way of the church is not to condemn anyone for eternity. It is to pour out the balm of God's mercy on all those who ask for it with a sincere heart"

All Christians seem to be shocked that Pope Francis appears to embrace the doctrine of Anonymous Christianity. Using scripture from the Gospel of Mark, Pope Francis recently explained to the listening audience of Vatican Radio how upset Jesus' disciples were that someone outside their group was doing good.

"They complain," the Pope said in his homily, because they say, "If he is not one of us, he cannot do good. If he is not of our party, he cannot do good." And Jesus corrects them: "Do not hinder him, he says, let him do good." The disciples, Pope Francis explains, "were a little intolerant," closed off by the idea of possessing the truth, convinced that "those who do not have the truth, cannot do good." "This was wrong . . . Jesus broadens the horizon." The Holy Father said, "The root of this possibility of doing good—that we all have—is in creation."

So, anonymous Christianity is the inclusive theological concept that declares that people who have never heard the Christian Gospel or interiorized it might be saved through Christ. The anonymous Christian is the person who has never had a true encounter with Christianity or Christ. Yet, God has moved this person's heart, and this person has responded positively to God and humanity in love. Hence, this person is in a graced state. But he or she does not really know it.

There is an old saying attributed to and identified with St. Francis of Assisi. It is a wonderful saying for any of us to interiorize as it reflects the spirit of both St. Francis and Pope Francis:

> "Preach the Gospel at all times. Use words if necessary."

ANONYMOUS CHRISTIANITY; KARL RAHNER, S. J., AND VATICAN II

Much of the inspiration for the idea of anonymous Christianity comes from the Second Vatican Council documents which teaches:

> "Those who through no fault of their own, do not know the Gospel of Christ or His Church, but who nevertheless seek God with a sincere heart, moved by grace, try in their actions to do His will as they know it through the dictates of their conscience . . . those too may achieve eternal salvation" (Vatican Council II, *Lumen Gentium*, 28).

> "One is the community of all peoples, one their origin, for God made the whole human race to live over the face of the earth. One also is their final goal, God" (Vatican Council II, *Nostra Aetate* 1).

> "there is a growing awareness of the exalted dignity proper to the human person, since he stands above all things, and his rights and duties are universal and inviolable" (Vatican Council II, *Gaudium et Spes* 26).

> "Likewise, other religions found everywhere try to counter the restlessness of the human heart, each in its own manner, by proposing 'ways,' comprising teachings, rules of life, and sacred rites. The Catholic Church rejects nothing that is true and holy in these religions. She regards with sincere reverence those ways of conduct and of life, those precepts and teachings which, though differing in many aspects from the ones she holds and sets forth, nonetheless often reflect a ray of that Truth which enlightens all men. Indeed, she proclaims, and ever must proclaim Christ 'the way, the truth, and the life' (John 14:6), in whom men may find the fullness of religious life, in whom God has reconciled all things to Himself" (Vatican Council II, *Nostra Aetate* 2).

Much of the thinking behind Vatican II concerning anonymous Christianity came from the writings of the modern Catholic theologian, Karl Rahner, S.J. He was behind much of the theology that flowed from the Council documents. He maintained that because God's salvific will is universal, there should exist at least a possibility for all persons to be saved. As was stated previously, his theology was called "Transcendental Anthropology" as Rahner believed that within the human person exists the longing and capacity for transcendence. Rahner believed strongly that we must understand the religious "other." In Rahner's *Foundations* (176), he presents his doctrine of the "anonymous Christian." He maintains that the Hindu, Buddhist, or Moslem, for example, may well accept what Christianity wants to convey. Rahner suggests that this can happen in an evolutionary spiritual process without that Hindu, Buddhist, or Moslem professing a Christian faith. Rahner posits that whenever a person accepts God's call to transcendence and responds to it, one becomes a Christian (anonymously), even perhaps without knowing the name of Christ, being baptized, or professing any doctrines or dogmas of the Christian religion. Quoting Rahner:

> "Christianity does not simply confront the member of an extra-Christian religion as a mere non-Christian, but as someone who can and must already be regarded in this or that respect as an anonymous Christian" (Rahner, *Karl Rahner In Dialogue*, 131).

Also:

> "Anonymous Christianity means that a person lives in the grace of God and attains salvation outside of explicitly constituted Christianity — Let us say, a Buddhist monk — who, because he follows his conscience, attains salvation and lives in the grace of God; of him I must say that he is an anonymous Christian; if not, I would have to presuppose that there is a genuine path to salvation that really attains that goal, but that simply has nothing to do with Jesus Christ. But I cannot do that. And so, if I hold if everyone depends upon Jesus Christ for salvation, and if at the same time I hold that many live in the world who have not expressly recognized Jesus Christ, then there remains in my opinion nothing else but to take up this postulate of an anonymous Christianity" (Rahner, *Karl Rahner In Dialogue,* 135).

Karl Rahner in 1969, declared that the Second Vatican Council marked the beginning of the Catholic Church's self-recognition that it was, in fact, a "World Church." He identified three great epochs of the church's history. The first was a very short period in the early church when it saw itself as only Jewish-Christian. The second was the time it became a Hellenistic-European and Western church which lasted up until the time of Vatican II. It was At Vatican II that the Catholic Church began its transition from being a Western Church to becoming a World Church. Only a World Church of God in Christ could eventually become a Catholic church, truly universal; inclusive of Anonymous Christians.

Rahner, in his writings, never called for an end to Christian mission and evangelization, he only described that which might be possible due to the grace and goodness of a loving God who wants all to be saved and whose offer of salvation is universal. To sum up anonymous Christianity then: as humans, we are transcendental beings and the aim of our being is beyond all that we know, believe, and to which we respond. Hence, the endpoint of humanity and history, the Omega point, is not really the Christian faith. The end point is beyond the Church, beyond Christianity, beyond all the names and persons who we categorize in this world. Jesus Christ is much bigger than Christianity and it is Jesus Christ, the Universal Christ, who is the Omega Point. He is the Revelation of God beyond all comprehension of reason and logic. The fate of all professed Christians and all so-called anonymous Christians is totally and ultimately in the hands of Jesus Christ.

It first depends on the grace we have been given as a member of the human community and our response to it. Beyond that, it all depends on the Universal Christ who meets all of us at the Omega point at the end of time and history. At the Omega point, when we meet the Universal Christ and have the final opportunity to recognize him as the One True God, we will no longer, in any way, have the opportunity to remain 'anonymous.'

I consider Mahatma Gandhi, for example, to have been another one of those anonymous Christians. Although he did not profess that Jesus Christ was his Lord and savior during his earthly journey, his life exemplified the true meaning of what being a Christian was all about. He lived out the Gospel message without explicitly declaring himself a Christian. In fact, on one occasion, Gandhi was asked why he had never become a Christian. His answer was, at the same time, both profound and revelatory. He replied, "Because I never met a Christian." Certainly Gandhi had met those who professed to be Christian during his lifetime; however, he believed that he had never truly met anyone who was living an authentic Christian life. To his mind, he had never met anyone who reflected the aura of real Christian Love; the *agape* love of God. It gave some indication of just how highly Gandhi thought of Christ and of true Christianity. Gandhi, being a good Hindu, believed in many gods. However, most Hindus do believe that there is a supreme God called "Brahma." Brahma is an entity without beginning or end, believed to inhabit every portion of reality and existence throughout the entire universe.

At the end of time, all names, terms, words, and definitions will be meaningless. God will be found in silence. There will be for us only the radiant peace of God's face. As all of humanity moves toward the Omega point, and we are all drawn into the Universal Christ; Gandhi, the anonymous Christian, will then meet a true Christian when he rises to meet Jesus Christ at the Omega Point. At that point, there will no longer be any need for searching, unknowing or anonymity.

Chapter Nineteen

"Being Saved,"
Now and at the End Times
(A Catholic's Understanding)

SALVATION, SIN, AND DEATH

Salvation is sometimes referred to as either redemption or deliverance. Salvation, in a scriptural sense, can be seen as liberation from perilous circumstances, death and damnation, or from sin and evil. Salvation is a pivotal point in life's drama and a key part of a script that was written before the world began. The end result for us will be a gift of freedom and security. As sin is the greatest evil; being the root of all evil, Sacred Scripture most often uses the word "salvation" or the implication of our "being saved" mainly in the sense of liberation from sin and its consequences. This is because in the Bible, sin is seen to ultimately end in death. Paul's Letter to the Romans tells us:

"The wages of sin is death" (Rom. 6:23).

SALVATION IS A PROCESS

The play of life has proven to be a very costly one. God's offer of salvation through Jesus Christ is universal; it is freely offered to everyone without exception. Although salvation is freely offered to all universally, it did come, however, at a terrible price. Only a free act of the will which rejects the offer of the grace of salvation can impede God's saving designs. So, saving us now and at the end of times for all eternity is the mission of our Lord and "Saviour" Jesus Christ. Salvation will not be fully completed until the Last Judgment, when the Second Coming of Christ would mark the catastrophic end of the world. Salvation is believed to be a process that continues through a person's life and is completed when they stand before Christ in judgment. Therefore, according to Catholic apologist James Akin, the faithful Christian can say in faith and hope, "I have been saved; I am being saved; and I will be saved."

SALVATION, THE INCARNATION AND ATONEMENT

Christian faith is faith in the God of salvation who has been revealed to us in Jesus of Nazareth. God, in his deep and abiding love for humankind and in his infinite wisdom, saw that the most fitting way to save us for all eternity from sin as the greatest evil, was through the incarnation of Jesus Christ. At the Second Coming of Jesus Christ, the "last enemy" to be destroyed will be death, the consequences of sin (1 Cor. 15:26).

Through the incarnation and the resulting crucifixion and resurrection, in the fullness of time, Jesus, God's Son, became our Saviour. This is referred to as the atonement because Jesus' death on the cross was the once-for-all sacrifice that atoned for the sin of humanity. The atonement can best be seen as an "at-one-ment" with Jesus Christ to remove our sin. Sin is a universal predicament for humanity, and we all share in the stain of it. We have all sinned and fall short of the glory of God. As the Epistle of John tells us:

> "If we say that we have no sin, we deceive ourselves and the truth is not in us" (1 John 1:8).

As Saviour, by atoning for our sin and damnation and establishing truth and the Kingdom of God, he ultimately provided us with the Holy Spirit which proceeded from the Father and the Son. The Holy Spirit empowers us with the spiritual strength to struggle along with God against the powers of darkness and sin. We have been given a participating role in this universal struggle.

SALVATION, FAITH AND GRACE

It is through the grace of God and the Holy Spirit within us that our sinner's hearts can be stirred. We can thus believe in the power that Jesus Christ has to save us as we are called not only to firm belief in him and his Word, but also to sense the call to further conversion and repentance. This grace and the receiving of the Holy Spirit is not something which can be merited by us; it proceeds solely from the love and mercy of God. We, through our free choice, can either receive or reject this inspiration of God within us. We may either turn to God and be saved or remain in sin. But grace, however, will not interfere with our free will. If we reject the grace of God and remain in our sins, we risk damnation by freely separating ourselves from God. Turning to God in our free will implies that we detest our sins, accept God's grace and promised plan of salvation, and admit that we are in need of a Saviour. God, in his Divine Mercy, will then save us for Christ's sake.

However, as Christians it is faith in Jesus Christ which is necessary for our salvation. The Catholic Catechism tells us:

> "Believing in Jesus Christ and in the One who sent him for our salvation is necessary for obtaining that salvation. Since without faith, it is impossible to please God" (*Catechism* 161).

THE FULL REALIZATION OF BEING SAVED

Through Baptism, we as Christians share in God's plan of salvation even now. However, we still await the full realization of the impact of that salvation, the redemption of our bodies, and the receiving of a glorified body at the Second Coming of Christ. The full realization of our "being saved" must be deferred to the end of time and history as we know it. It is our hope, which cannot be our hope if its object is seen. The Apostle Paul's New Testament Letters tell us:

> "We ourselves have the first fruits of the Spirit, we also groan within ourselves as we wait for adoption, the redemption of our bodies. For in hope we were saved" (Rom. 8:24).

> "Our citizenship is in heaven and from it we also await a savior, the Lord Jesus Christ. He will change our lowly body, to conform with his glorified body" (Phil. 3:20–21).

In the New Testament world of commerce, a ransom was the price that was necessarily paid to buy back an object which had been pawned or the cost for liberating a slave and setting them free. In Jesus Christ's role as our Saviour, we are also being redeemed, i.e., literally "bought back" from the bondage of sin into the grace of God as the free gift of God.

SALVATION IS COMMUNAL

We are "being saved," not merely as individuals or in isolation, but salvation has a communal dimension. As part of Christ's church which is a Sacrament of the Kingdom of God, we are being saved because we are in communion with the people of God, as God in Christ, each one having a share of the one body and the same Holy Spirit. The Fathers of the Second Vatican Council expressed this in the following manner:

> "God did not create man for life in isolation but for the formation of social unity. So also, it has pleased God to make men holy and save them not merely as individuals, without any mutual bonds, but by making them into a single people, a people who acknowledges Him in truth and serves Him in holiness. So from the beginning of Salvation history, He has chosen men not just as individuals but as members of a certain community. Revealing His mind to them, God called these chosen ones 'His People' (Exod. 3:7–12), and, furthermore, made a covenant with them on Sinai" (Cf. Exod. 24:1–8)(Vatican Council II, *Gaudium Et Spes* 32).

SALVATION HISTORY

Salvation history is ongoing, and no one is excluded from at least the possibility of salvation. It is the universal offer of a loving God. The free acceptance of salvation is a gift of God's grace. Our "being saved" is a process planned at creation and begun with the death and resurrection of Jesus Christ, then ending at the Second Coming of Christ. It is the history of a relationship between God and humankind that was created by God, transformed by Christ, and is either accepted or rejected by us as human beings. In Salvation history, humankind is brought toward the Kingdom of God, first in Jesus Christ (the Kingdom in our midst and the mid- point) and finally and fully with the Second Coming.

The story of the universe, and everything that various and conflicting scientific theories can tell us about its long history, is part of a larger story, the story of salvation. Its history is incorporated into Salvation history as its converging ground. At the end of Salvation history, it will be the resurrected Jesus in his glorified body who comes to save us. The coming of the Universal Christ, our God-Hero, at the Omega Point will allow us to make more sense of the death of Jesus of Nazareth on the cross of Calvary at the mid-point of Salvation history. The Evangelist John, the Gospel writer tell us:

> "Amen, amen I say to you, unless a grain of wheat falls to the ground and dies, it remains just a grain of wheat; but if it dies, it produces much fruit" (John 12:24).

Salvation as a history is dynamic and is not exclusively in the future. It flows backwards and forward alike. Backward to its beginning at creation in its opening act, then all the way to the climactic midpoint in Jesus' death and resurrection and ultimately forward to its final act at the Second Coming when the Universal Christ; the Resurrected Christ, comes to save us. As part of Salvation history, we cannot view our salvation apart from looking at the

Universal Christ, the Pre-Existent Christ, and the Christ of Calvary. Our salvation will have not only personal, but supreme universal implications.

For the time being, in the now moment, it is enough to have the hope of Christ within us of our "being saved" at the end of time and history at the Omega Point. The Apostle Paul tells us:

> "For in hope we were saved. Now hope that sees for itself is not hope. For who hopes for what one sees? But if we hope for what we do not see, we wait with endurance" (Rom. 8:24–25).

The Holy Spirit within us is our pledge that this hope of salvation will be realized by God. Finally, I do believe in God's promise of salvation, because it was offered not just for my sake but more so for Christ's sake, God's Hero; my Hero.

Most every play has a climax. As was stated earlier, the climactic moment of all history is the event of Jesus Christ. This will always be the pre-eminent "sign of the times." This makes the ending not just linear, but circular. The end is in the beginning and the beginning is in the end. In the incarnation of Jesus Christ, the predictable ending to this play of life was replaced as there developed a new twist, a surprise ending. Death as an ending was set aside and the play was rewritten with a new ending-to include those resurrected and bound for glory along with Jesus Christ. Because all history has become parallel with salvation history, we will one day with all the Saints be able to repeat the words of Jesus on the cross and say, "It is finished" (John 19:30).

"Everything will be perfect in the end.
If it's not perfect, it's not the end."
—*Version of a modern aphorism*

ω

Bibliography

Akin, James; *The Salvation Controversy*. San Diego, CA: Catholic Answers Publications, 2001.

Aquinas, Thomas. *The "Summa Theologica" of St. Thomas Aquinas*.Trans. Fathers of the English Dominican Province. London: Burns, Oates & Washburne, 1920. Web. 09 Dec. 2015. http://newadvent.org/summa/index.html.

Aristotle. *Nichomachean Ethics*. Trans. W.D. Ross. The Internet Classics Archive. Web. 09 Dec. 2015. http://classics.mit.edu/aristotle/nichomachean.5.v.html.

———. *Physics*. Trans. Hardie and Gaye. The Internet Classics Archive. Web. 09 Dec. 2015. http://classics.mit.edu/Aristotle/Physics.4.iv.htm.

Beckwith, Ryan Teague. "Transcript: Read the Speech Pope Francis Gave to Congress." *Time* . Time Inc, 24 Sept. 2015. Web. 10 Dec. 2015. http://time.com/4048176/pope-francis-us-visit-congress-transcript/.

Boethius. *Consolations of Philosophy*. Trans. W.V. Cooper. London: J.M. Dent and Company, 1902. Web.

Brown, Raymond, Joseph Fitzmeyer, and Roland Murphy. *The New Jerome Biblical Commentary*. Englewood Cliffs, NJ: Prentice Hall Publishing, 1990. Print.

Catechism of the Catholic Church. New Hope, Ky: Urbi et Orbi Communications, 1994. Print.

"Correctional Populations in the United States." *Bureau of Justice Statistics (BJS)* . Web. 10 Dec. 2015. http://www.bjs.gov/index.cfm?ty=pbse&sid=5.

de Chardin, Pierre Teilhard. *Divine Milieu*. New York, NY: Harper Perennial/Harper Collins, 1960.

———. *Le Christique*. Paris, France: Contemporary French Fiction Publishing, 1955.

———. *Science and Christ*. New York, NY: Harper & Row, 1968.

———. *The Future of Man*. New York, NY: Harper Perennial/Harper Collins, 1959.

———. *The Heart of Matter*. New York, NY: Harcourt Brace Jovanovich, 1979.

———. *The Phenomenon of Man*. New York, NY: Harper Perennial/Harper Collins, 1965.

De Smedt, Charles. "Historical Criticism." The Catholic Encyclopedia. Vol. 4. New York: Robert Appleton Company, 1908. 10 Dec. 2015 http://www.newadvent.org/cathen/04503a.htm.

Delany, Joseph. "Corporal and Spiritual Works of Mercy." The Catholic Encyclopedia. Vol. 10. New York: Robert Appleton Company, 1911. 10 Dec. 2015 http://www.newadvent.org/cathen/10198d.htm.

Dods, Marcus, trans. From *Nicene and Post-Nicene Fathers*, First Series, Vol. 2. Edited by Philip Schaff. (Buffalo, NY: Christian Literature Publishing Co., 1887.) Revised and edited for New Advent by Kevin Knight. http://www.newadvent.org/fathers/120120.htm.

"Finding God in All Things." *Ignatian Spirituality* . Jesuits.org, n.d. Web. 10 Dec. 2015. http://
jesuits.org/spirituality.

Foley, Mark. *Story of a Soul: The Autobiography of St. Therese of Lisieux.* Washington, DC:
Institute of Carmelite Studies Publishing, 2005.

Garrigou-LaGrange, Reginald. "La Providence et la confiance en Dieu." Theology of Providence. Rockford, IL: Tan Publishing 1998. Print.

Gigot, Francis. "Biblical Introduction." The Catholic Encyclopedia. Vol. 8. New York: Robert
Appleton Company, 1910. 10 Dec. 2015 http://www.newadvent.org/cathen/08078b.htm.

"Hail Mary." OurCatholicPrayers.com. Web. http://www.ourcatholicprayers.com/the-saint-mi-
chael-prayer.html.

Hardon, John A. *The Catholic Catechism* . Garden City, NY: Doubleday, 1975. Print.

Heschel, Abraham. "The Holy Dimension." *Essential Works; Correspondence.* Maryknoll,
NY: Orbis Books, 2011.

———. *God In Search Of Man.* New York, NY: Farrar, Straus & Cudahy, 1955.

Holweck, Frederick. "St. Michael the Archangel." The Catholic Encyclopedia. Vol. 10. New
York: Robert Appleton Company, 1911. 10 Dec. 2015 http://www.newadvent.org/cathen/
10275b.htm.

Johnson, Richard F. *Saint Michael the Archangel.* Woodbridge, Suffolk, UK: Boydell Press,
2005.

Kirsch, Johann Peter. "Millennium and Millenarianism." The Catholic Encyclopedia. Vol. 10.
New York: Robert Appleton Company, 1911. 10 Dec. 2015 http://www.newadvent.org/
cathen/10307a.htm.

LaHaye, Tim. *Bible Prophecy; the Left Behind Series.* Carol Stream, IL: Tyndale Publishing,
1995.

———. *The Beginning of the End.* Carol Stream, IL: Tyndale Publishing, 1972).

Lebreton, Jules. "St. Justin Martyr." The Catholic Encyclopedia. Vol. 8. New York: Robert
Appleton Company, 1910. 9 Dec. 2015 http://www.newadvent.org/cathen/08580c.htm.

Lindsey, Hal; *The Late Great Planet Earth.* New York, NY: Bantam Books/Random House,
1970.

Longley, Robert. "U.S. Prison and Jail Population Tops 2 Million." *News & Issues* .
About.com, 8 Apr. 2003. Web. 10 Dec. 2015. http://usgovinfo.about.com/cs/censusstatistic/
a/aaprisonpop.htm.

Martens, John. "The Challenge of the Word." *America Magazine.* Ed. Bernard Lonergan. New
York, NY: America Media, 2015.

McElwee, Joshua. "Pope Tells Vatican Theological Commission to Respect Diverse Views."
National Catholic Reporter . N.p., 5 Dec. 2014. Web. 10 Dec. 2015. http://ncronline.org/
news/theology/pope-tells-vatican-theological-commission-respect-diverse-views.

"Mercy." *Online Etymology Dictionary.* Ed. Douglas Harper. Web. 10 Dec. 2015. http://
www.etymonline.com/index.php?search=mercy&searchmode=none.

Michaud, Derek. "Karl Rahner (1904-1984)." *Boston Collaborative Encyclopedia of Western
Theology* . N.p., n.d. Web. 10 Dec. 2015. http://people.bu.edu/wwildman/bce/rahner.htm.

Mooney, Christopher. *Teilhard de Chardin and the Mystery of Christ.* New York, NY: Harper
& Row, 1966.

Newman, John Henry. *Magnificat Magazine.* 11 December 2015: 149. Print.

O'Connell, Gerard. "Pope Francis Declares A Jubilee Year of Mercy." *America Magazine* .
The National Catholic Review, 18 Mar. 2015. Web. 10 Dec. 2015. http://americamaga-
zine.org/issue/pope-francis-declares-jubilee-year-mercy.

Pasquini, John. "Gandhi." *The Existence of God: Convincing and Converging Arguments.*
Lanham, MD: University Press of America, 2010.

Pilkington, J.G., trans. From *Nicene and Post-Nicene Fathers,* First Series, Vol. 1. Edited by
Philip Schaff. (Buffalo, NY: Christian Literature Publishing Co., 1887.) Revised and edited
for New Advent by Kevin Knight. http://www.newadvent.org/fathers/110101.htm.

Plato. *Timaeus.* Trans. Benjamin Jowett. The Internet Classics Archive. Web. 09 Dec. 2015.
http://classics.mit.edu/Plato/timaeus.html.

Pohlen, Tony. "Reflection." *FaithND* . MyNotreDame, 22 Apr. 2015. Web. 10 Dec. 2015. http://faith.nd.edu/s/1210/faith/social.aspx?sid=1210&gid=609&pgid=24551&cid=47267&ecid=47267&crid=0&calpgid=10745&calcid=24190.

"Pope at Mass: Culture of Encounter Is the Foundation of Peace." Vatican Radio, 22 May 2013. Web. 10 Dec. 2015. http://en.radiovaticana.va/storico/2013/05/22/pope_at_mass_culture_of_encounter_is_the_foundation_of_peace/en1-694445.

Pope Benedict XVI. "On the Meaning of Death: With Christ, it Has Been Deprived of its Venom." Vatican City, IT. 6 November 2006. Papal Address.

Pope Francis I. Joy of the Gospel: *Apostolic Exhortation, Evangelii Gaudium, of the Holy Father Francis to the Bishops, Clergy, Consecrated Persons and the Lay Faithful on the Proclamation of the Gospel in Today's World*. Rome, Italy. 24 Nov. 2013. Web.

———. "Reading the Signs of the Times." Homily at Casa San Marta. Nov. 2013. *Catholic News Agency* . Web. 09 Dec. 2015.

———. "Synod on the Family Address." Vatican City, IT. 24 October 2015. Papal Address.

———. *Laudato Si, On Care for Our Common Home*. May 2013. Dec. 8, 2015. http://www.papalencyclicals.net.

Pope John Paul II. *To Set Fire on the Earth*. Yonkers, NY: Magnificat Publications, 2015.

Pope John XXIII. "See, judge, act." *Mater et MaGistra*. May 1961. Dec. 8, 2015. http://www.papalencyclicals.net/john23/j23mater.htm.

Pope Leo XIII. "Prayer to St. Michael." *Leonide Prayers After Low Mass*. OurCatholicPrayers.com. 1884. Web. http://www.ourcatholicprayers.com/the-saint-michael-prayer.html.

Pope Pious IX. *Dives In Misericordia Deus*. February 14, 1877. December 2, 2015. http://papalencyclicals.net/ereader.htm.

Rahner, Karl. "Time." *Encyclopedia of Theology: The Concise Sacramentum Mundi* . New York: Seabury, 1975. N. pag. Print.

———. "Anonymous Christians." *Foundations of Christian Faith.*New York, NY: Seabury Press, 1978.

———. "Supernatural Existential." *Foundations of Christian Faith.*New York, NY: Seabury Press, 1978.

———. "Towards a Fundamental Theological Interpretation of Vatican II." *Theological Studies*, 40. 1979.

———. "Transcendental Anthropology." *Foundations of Christian Faith.*New York, NY: Seabury Press, 1978.

———. *Encounters With Silence*. Westminster, MD: Newman Press, 1960.

———. *Karl Rahner in Dialogue*. Ed. Imhof, Biallowons, and Egan. New York, NY: Crossroads Publishing, 1986.

———. *Theological Investigations*. London: Darton, Longman & Todd, 1961. Web. http://www.librarything.com/work/5420792.

Reid, George. "Biblical Criticism (Higher)." The Catholic Encyclopedia. Vol. 4. New York: Robert Appleton Company, 1908. 10 Dec. 2015 http://www.newadvent.org/cathen/04491c.htm.

Rich, Tracey R. "Tzedakah: Charity." *Judaism 101* . N.p., 2011. Web. 10 Dec. 2015. http://www.jewfaq.org/tzedakah.htm.

Saint Joseph Edition of the New American Bible. New York: Catholic Book Pub. Co, 1970. Print.

Sammon, Sean D. "The Birth of the World Church." *America Magazine* . The National Catholic Review, 15 Oct. 2012. Web. 10 Dec. 2015. http://www.americamedia.org/issue/100/birth-world-church.

Seven Themes of Catholic Social Teaching." United States Conference of Catholic Bishops. N.p., 2005. Web. 10 Dec. 2015. http://www.usccb.org/beliefs-and-teachings/what-we-believe/catholic-social-teaching/seven-themes-of-catholic-social-teaching.cfm.

Shakespeare, William. *As You Like It*. 1598. Web. 10 Dec. 2015. http://shakespeare.mit.edu/asyoulikeit/full.html.

———. *Merchant of Venice*. 1596. Web. 10 Dec. 2015. http://shakespeare.mit.edu/merchant/merchant.4.1.html.

Sollier, Joseph. "Supernatural Order." The Catholic Encyclopedia. Vol. 14. New York: Robert Appleton Company, 1912. 10 Dec. 2015 http://www.newadvent.org/cathen/14336b.htm.

Stedman, Ray C. "Ch 9: Time and Eternity." *RayStedman.org: Authentic Christianity* . Ray Stedman Ministries, 2010. Web. 10 Dec. 2015. http://www.raystedman.org/authentic-Christianity/time-and-eternity.

Sullivan, James. "The Athanasian Creed." The Catholic Encyclopedia. Vol. 2. New York: Robert Appleton Company, 1907. 10 Dec. 2015 http://www.newadvent.org/cathen/02033b.htm.

The Lord's Prayer." OurCatholicPrayers.com. Web. http://www.ourcatholicprayers.com.

Theresa of Avila. "Interior Castle." *Magnificat Meditation*. Yonkers, NY: Magnificat, 2015. Web. http://www.ccel.org/ccel/teresa/castle2.html.

Thurston, Herbert. "Apostles' Creed." The Catholic Encyclopedia. Vol. 1. New York: Robert Appleton Company, 1907. 10 Dec. 2015 http://www.newadvent.org/cathen/01629a.htm.

———. "Hail Mary." The Catholic Encyclopedia. Vol. 7. New York: Robert Appleton Company, 1910. 10 Dec. 2015 http://www.newadvent.org/cathen/07110b.htm.

———. "The Lord's Prayer." The Catholic Encyclopedia. Vol. 9. New York: Robert Appleton Company, 1910. 10 Dec. 2015 http://www.newadvent.org/cathen/09356a.htm.

"Transcend." *Online Etymology Dictionary*. Ed. Douglas Harper. Web. 10 Dec. 2015. http://www.etymonline.com/index.php?term=transcend&allowed_in_frame=0.

Vatican Council II: The Conciliar and Post Conciliar Documents. Ed. Austin Flannery. Wilmington, Del: Scholarly Resources, 1975. Print.

Wesley, C. "453." The Communion of Saints; *Book of Hymns for Public and Private Devotion ; Evangelical Lutheran Hymnbook* St. Louis: Concordia Publishing, 1918. 8 December 2015. Web. www.hymnary.org/hymn/bhppd866/453.

Wilhelm, Joseph. "The Nicene Creed." The Catholic Encyclopedia. Vol. 11. New York: Robert Appleton Company, 1911. 10 Dec. 2015 http://www.newadvent.org/cathen/11049a.htm.

Zimmerman, Benedict. "St. John of the Cross." The Catholic Encyclopedia. Vol. 8. New York: Robert Appleton Company, 1910. 8 Dec. 2015.

Index

About the Author

Michael Hickey is a graduate of Northeastern University, Boston, MA., and a Master Of Divinity Studies graduate of Weston Jesuit, Cambridge, MA., The Boston College School of Theology and Ministry.

Following a career as a corporate executive for a Fortune 500 company, he became a Director of two 501 C-3 charitable non-profits; he was Executive Director of Food For The Poor Inc., Deerfield Beach, Fl., and Development Director for My Brother's Table Soup Kitchen, Lynn, MA. When he began to approach retirement, he began his own marketing business, retiring as a successful entrepreneur in his late fifties to teach and write.

He has had 3 works previously published; GET WISDOM, GET GOODNESS, and GET REAL. The former was self-published and the latter two books were published by University Press of America/ Rowman & Littlefield Publishing Co., Lanham, MD.

He is married to Theresa, a published poet, and in their fifty years of marriage they have raised four happy and "well adjusted" children into adulthood.

GET TΩ THE END is his most recent book.